From Dust to Discipline

Achieve Your Fullest Potential

Copyright © 2020 by Nastassia Ponomarenko

From Dust to Discipline

ISBN for this edition: 978-0-578-62639-0

Book formatting by: **Last Mile Publishing**

First Edition Published: February, 2020

Dedication

I dedicate this book to all of the wonderful people who are reading it. I especially have so much empathy towards young adults, so my dedication is targeted towards all of you. Reading books has significantly bettered me, so I hope this book at least inspires you to start becoming your best self. Each and every single one of us has the potential to live our happiest and most successful lives, so let's get to it.

Acknowledgement

Thank you to all of my followers and friends who have supported me and continue to support me throughout my transformation of becoming my best self.

Thank you to those who doubted my potential of even writing a book. I hope some things in here will be eye-opening for you.

Most importantly, thank You God. I cried out to You in desperation in summer 2018, and You accepted me. I went back into Your arms, and You began working through me.

Table of Contents

Introduction

Being at a certain age should not deem anyone more or less capable of doing something. Life and life's wisdom approach each person differently. A man could be 50 and still act foolish, just like a young man can be in his early 20's and possess a certain level of knowledge and maturity that surpasses the expectations one has for that age.

So, I want to ask you of two things: please do not hold bias while reading this because of my age, and please read this book with an open mind. So many of us tend to shut ourselves off from really hearing the things that may be outside of our comfort zone, but these beliefs might be enough to change our whole life around in a positive way.

I wrote this book to serve you in improving your life in every aspect and to partially share my story. The title *From Dust to Discipline,* symbolizes a significant transformation, leaving behind the past that held me to mediocrity and embarking on the challenging path of constantly trying to be better within the mental, physical, spiritual and emotional realms.

I believe it will be of great service to many people, especially since most of us have set beliefs that were ingrained in our heads since we were young. Whether it was from our parents, our society, or our friends, we were told how to act, who we need to be, and what we should believe. Some of these may be positive, but unfortunately, an overwhelming majority of us get told the wrong things, resulting in broken mindsets, broken hearts, and deep wounds. Set these preconceived notions aside and open your mind. If you do this, I swear your life will change significantly.

In order for change to occur, a deep dive into personal topics and stories that go beyond the surface level need to be made. I was lucky enough to find some of the greatest self-improvement books at a young age of 18, and through this, I have learned life-changing principles and Truths. Books from the most profound authors such as Napoleon Hill, Oprah, Deepak Chopra, Don Miguel Ruiz, and many more. A significant quote that always sticks with me is "The person you will become in 5 years is based on the books you read and the people you surround yourself with today" - Ruben Chavez. Accurate. Make sure to highlight this and other quotes along the way, they ring a lot of truth!

Take this from me. In the span of one year, I have changed my entire life around. Through all of the books I read, the level of awareness, intellect and wisdom that I received is absolutely incredible. I have eliminated people that were halting my journey of growth and began to surround myself with positive and uplifting influences. Some people really think that what we do, watch, and spend our time on have no effect on ourselves when it is the complete opposite. Even if it is to a small degree, everything we do transmits energy.

My book is essentially self-improvement mixed with an autobiography, and my goal is to help lead you to your highest potential as an individual in this chaotic and overstimulated world. With that being said, here we go!

Chapter 1

Addressing a Misconception

Most people only see the "now" and never experience what actually happened in the past, behind closed doors, that got them there. Of course, this is totally normal and to be expected. They see their current physique, their materialistic possessions, knowledge, "success," etc. I put success in quotes because I do not classify myself as successful, but I do acknowledge that I have achieved many amazing things thus far in my life. I am still on my lifelong journey, and I still have years to acquire more knowledge and skill. This is why it is extremely monumental for me to talk and show the journey to success.

My definition of success has been evolving and is much more evolved than it used to be. In the past, success meant having a bank account in the millions, engaging with millions of people, having multi-million businesses, and being happy. My current definition is a little different. I had an eye-opening experience in early 2019 about money and status. I strived to make x amount of money, and I asked myself, "What is my intent for getting this money? Why do I have this goal?" It came down to reasons that weren't beneficial to me, so I quickly gave up my fixation on economic success, because it served no purpose to my soul.

For me, success is doing everything I love to do every day, being great at it, and maintaining a level of peace, joy and happiness simultaneously. I want to live in the way God intends me to live. Acquiring money is just a bonus, one that will help give me freedom and more opportunities to create and to give on a higher level. I have come to realize that life really is simple, and it's the simple things that are the most fulfilling. I long to fulfill my soul, and I try to do so by working daily on my spirituality and relationship with God, creating meaningful content, seeing everyone and everything in the eyes of love, and going out of my comfort zone and breaking free from any mental boundaries. To me, this is a crucial part of my definition of success. And, oh man, it's hard, but so extremely rewarding. I have tasted bits and pieces of my version of success, and it is the most delicious and satisfying feeling ever.

We often only hear about the successes of others, but don't always know what it took to get there. Unless someone posts every single moment of their life on social media, most things happen behind closed doors. Blood, sweat, and tears are all a part of it. The journey to self-improvement and success is very, very hard, and it does not become easy if the main goal is to constantly reach out of the comfort zone. Humans are absolute pros at adapting to challenges and hardship. It's quite amazing., and it's quite a skill to constantly challenge yourself. The toughest days are the ones that ultimately mold our character and mindset. *tru.*

The first thing that I did to improve myself was when I started getting into fitness. I have been athletic for most of my life playing soccer and basketball and doing gymnastics and track and field, but this was much different than any sport. I was a second-semester freshman in High School and was 15 ½ when I unknowingly found my greatest passion at that time. It started quite simply. I was scrolling through Instagram and came across a couple of fitness models that really inspired me. I had no clue what workouts to do, so I did my research and began from there. All I knew was that I had this burning desire in me to get fit.

My parents did not support nor understand my obsession for the gym because it was so out of their realm of expectations for me, which did create some drama, chaos, arguments and tears. I battled this until I graduated from High School. Like I said, I had a burning desire to get fit, so a couple of opinions and naysayers wouldn't stop me. I will never forget the day my dad and I got an argument when he took away all of my shoes (except my flip flops), so I couldn't go to the gym. As a result, I Ubered to the mall, bought a glittery pair of Converse and walked myself to the gym to train my lower body! No obligatory leg days skipped! #dedication

I really don't know where I get my drive and determination from. I assume that it is partially genetics and partially how I was raised. I apply this drive to anything I truly and wholeheartedly want to accomplish, not even caring whether I will fail, embarrass myself, or get judged. Because of my strong will and stubbornness, that's why I am where I am.

Let's talk a little bit about money. Some people tend to shy away from talking about it for various reasons, but this shouldn't be something that is shunned. Money is not the root of all evil; the evil starts as soon as money becomes misused and abused just like how many God-given things are in life.

I certainly do not share the same views about money as I did some time ago. My eyes are now focused on creating as much change in the area I am most passionate about, which is why I wrote this book in the first place. I used to have a selfish and prideful way of seeing money and materialistic possessions, but now I see it much differently, and I am so grateful for my change in perspective. The wrong perspective will make anyone slaves to money for the never-ending pursuit of more, more, and more. I will talk about this more in later chapters.

Onto the subject of discipline. This is one of the most important "things" people need to master to be successful. Discipline is doing x, y, and z when you don't feel like doing it. It's persevering through something that's challenging and needs to be overcome. Most people do not realize it took so much work behind closed doors to practice and instill. There were and still are days I didn't want to go to the gym, pray, read, work on my business, wake up early, eat clean, the list goes on. Discipline is a skill that is applied daily and not when someone "feels like it," which is what the majority of people fall into. A feeling is fleeting, but discipline stays with you forever if you upkeep it. People want to be successful, but do not want it bad enough when they realize the number of sacrifices needed to get there. Remember, "if you want to be the best, you have to do the things that other people aren't willing to do." One of the distinct separations between the extremely successful and the rest of the population is exactly that; doing the things you don't feel like doing.

These are just a few attributes that people see. Through this, some even become discouraged and quit. That discouragement may lead to buying fit teas, weight loss pills, or getting surgery to enhance a certain part of the body that one is insecure about. This is what is pushed by industries and societal expectations. These are considered quick and easy solutions to avoid taking the hard route. Cha-ching! It's a very tempting mindset to be in, I get it.

But it isn't rewarding, because it isn't real, and is only utilized to make money from the people who do not want to put the proper work in. Whether you put in the work or not will decide whether you will win or lose. If you are looking for an easy way out, you have already lost. The struggle is what makes us mentally stronger, God puts every single thing that happens to us for a reason, especially the obstacles we face and overcome.

Chapter 2

My Past

"You have to make mistakes to find out who you aren't. You take the action, and the insight follows: You don't think your way into becoming yourself."
--Anne Lamott

In order for you to understand who I am today, you must know certain parts about my past. We will get to all of the inspirational stuff soon, I promise.

I grew up in a middle-class family of four with traditional Belarusian parents. I had a good childhood, as far as I can remember, but like most people, I also recall times where I had been failed. There's no other way to put it, and it isn't anyone's fault. We all make mistakes and (hopefully) learn from them. Regardless of what was said and done, I absolutely love my parents and they truly did a lot for me.

Thanks to my dad, I was athletic and played sports most of my life, which he supported me with by cheering me on and going to many of my games. I spent many years at different points of my life doing gymnastics, soccer, basketball, and track and field. My dad and I also share similar humor, so that makes us bond even more. Long story short, I am definitely a daddy's girl.

My mom physically nurtured me and took care of me. A turning point in my life was when she saw me failing in seventh grade, she took a leap of faith and put me in a Catholic school, which did wonders for me. Due to me wanting to continue a Catholic education, she also paid for four years of my High School tuition, which helped to mold me into the young woman that I have become today. Without that, I can only guess how I would've turned out. Overall, my parents' primary concerns were my health, education and grades, or so it seemed.

For me to show you why I behaved the way I did, I have to be open and honest. Despite being physically present, my parents really lacked in being emotionally supportive, understanding, and giving me advice as a young girl. Any time I went to them when I was vulnerable and sad, I was told that I was being "dramatic for no reason." Hearing that always hurt me. To be denied of my feelings at an early age really impacted me as a child. Because of that, I was always emotionally suppressed, especially around my parents. Any experience that I wanted to share would turn into a lecture that eventually turned into an argument. Ultimately, this would result in me not trusting my very own parents with things that would happen in my life. There were so many times when I told them something and left with the "ugh I shouldn't have told them anything to begin with."

Whenever I felt beautiful and would tell my parents about it, the response I would usually get went along the lines of "no, you are average." Hearing this broke me and unknowingly impacted me. I had no self-love instilled in me, and this created many problems down the line. I later confronted my dad about this and he said it was to "humble me" and because "it was true." I so longed for affectionate, accepting and loving words from my family, but it always seemed like I was never good enough just being me. Every young girl *needs* to hear that they are loved, beautiful, powerful, and protected. I so desperately wanted this. I wanted to be and to feel like I was accepted by my dad, and I so desperately craved my mom's advice, encouragement and emotional nurturing. I had two parents who were physically present but were extremely emotionally distant.

Throughout my entire life, I really wasn't good at making friends or at least the right kind of friends. I never had a clique I belonged to, and I constantly felt like I had to try extra hard just to make it seem like I wasn't a loner. Around the pre-teen and early teen time, I remember feeling lonely because I didn't have any close friends to hang out with and didn't know what to do with myself. Even though my elementary and middle school dream was to be popular (haven't put enough thought as to why I had this desire), I never really fit in. Let me put it into this perspective for you: I watched all of the most popular High School movie's made on Netflix just because I was so starstruck on the whole scene. It's ironic because these movies are nowhere close to how high school is in real life. So, as a little girl, I already showed signs of wanting attention, recognition, and the feeling of being important.

In terms of boys, I never really got their attention until somewhere in freshman year of high school. I kept trying to be like the girls that all the boys liked, and it just didn't work out at all. I was trying way too hard and began focusing on all of the wrong things. I think somewhere around 10 years old I even planned out how I will get a boyfriend by the age of 16 and how I am going to get a beautiful pink dress to wear at prom. My perception was out of order probably because of all the movies I watched as a kid. But hey, a little girl can dream!

Whether we like it or not, our childhood frames who we become as teenagers, young adults and adults, for better or worse. The way we were raised becomes engrained in our heads and subconsciously manifests itself into our behavior, thoughts and attitude. It's inevitable for that not to happen because these are the people, we spend most of our time with.

Chapter 3

My High School Years

I will do a quick recap of my years in high school.

Just to clarify, I went to public school for the majority of my education until my mom enrolled me in a Catholic school in eighth grade. Transferring over to a new school did wonders for me. I was surrounded by intelligent, friendly, supportive, and kind classmates and teachers. This experience gradually started influencing me to become a better overall person and to be more open-minded towards the possibility of God's existence.

When it was time for high school applications, I was rejected by a private Catholic school that I really wanted to get into (it actually happens to be the school I transferred to for Junior year). My weak reasoning for applying there was because it was a prestigious school with highly reputable teachers and education. And since my brother did graduate from there, why not just follow in his footsteps? Of course, there were other meaningful reasons, but they didn't matter to me as much as the status of the school I would be attending.

It was quite discouraging to be rejected from the school that I wanted to get accepted into. It was yet another bullet point to add to my reasons as to why I felt like I wasn't good enough. My parents didn't really help with my self-confidence and only added more negative fuel to the fire with their words. It always seemed like I lacked something. Even though I didn't do badly in school, I was the "slowest" learner out of everyone in my family, and they reminded me of that all the time. I never had any learning disabilities, and I just needed more time to get something drilled into my head as opposed to my family understanding something almost immediately. Or so they claimed. I have a brother who is 9 years older than me, and I was often compared to him in the past. He obeyed everything my parents told him to do, achieved amazing grades, and went to a great college. And then there was me who earned the title of being destined for failure. Ha-ha. The fact of the matter is, I'm just different and being different is sometimes frowned upon. At least that is how it was in the beginning. It takes much more time, effort and a certain level of awareness to try to understand a person instead of scolding and quitting on them.

From what I know, it seems that many foreign parents do not seem to understand nor want to understand that their children are going to be different from them, no matter how much they want to preserve the values and cultures they were instilled with themselves. It's understandable, they were raised completely differently, so no one is at fault here. But each person's path in life is different, unique and only tailored to that individual. Someone might be gifted at memorizing formulas and applying them compared to someone who is more creative and naturally business minded. This does not mean that someone is better than the other, it just means that these two people are *unique* in their own way. Guess what? Our education system rewards the first type of student. Just as an example, the SAT's clearly don't care about someone starting a business to solve a societal issue or innovate something that serves a greater purpose to humanity. Why are we limiting people to mathematical problems and sentence structuring? As we all know, this test is a huge component of getting into a good college too.

So many people idolize straight A's, when having a perfect report card has little to no correlation with being successful outside of school walls. I believe that we are getting better at realizing this, but there is still a lot of misconceptions and stigmas. Many successful people, either dead or alive, had little to no schooling, dropped out of school, or did not have the greatest grades. Don't believe me? Spend two minutes researching this on Google. There's a great quote by Robert Kiyosaki saying, "'A' students work for 'C' students and 'B' students work for the government." Kiyosaki is essentially saying that those people who did not do as well in school became business owners or entrepreneurs and hired those who were top achievers in their class later on.

Of course, this doesn't apply to everyone, but it does ring some truth to it. Elon Musk graduated from college and was probably the best and brightest student in all of his classes, and he is a world changer. So it all really depends, but I can confidently say that from experience and by listening to other people, these educational systems do not propel anyone to a successful *and* happy life. We are left on our own to figure that out. Don't even get me started on taxes.

Anyway, I got accepted into a school where many of the other students also didn't get accepted into their first choice. During my time there, my parents did not fail to remind me that I was the "best of the worst" of my classmates. Yet another comment that left a strong mark on me. However, I actually really liked my school. Since we only had around 250 students in total, it was easy for me to get involved in anything I wanted to do. I participated in Tennis, Basketball, Track & Field, and was also involved in student government and campus ministry. All of these extracurricular activities were really fun and were overall a great experience to get out of my comfort zone with.

Introduction to Catholicism was a game-changing class for me and one that I am very grateful for. Because I was thrown into theology (study of God) in 8th grade, I never learned the basics and fundamentals of the faith. It's inexplicable what happened, but somewhere around my first semester I experienced a conversion. I genuinely prayed for the first time and something in me clicked. The doubt of God's existence went away, and I began feeling at peace, which I never felt before. It was beautiful.

Growing up, I had so much disbelief. You know, it was the whole, "If He is real, then why can't anybody see Him?" and "If God exists, why do we have all of this evil and suffering?" I had many questions left unanswered and didn't have any education about theology, so I didn't think much of Him. How could I if I wasn't aware and knew nothing? So because of that class, I truly felt and believed that God was very much alive and real for the first time in my life. Big, big change in my life. I was joyful, radiant, and peaceful.

Sophomore Year

I can't quite find the words to describe exactly what Sophomore year was like for me. I guess one way to put it would be: an abuse of freedom and total negligence of my moral compass and intuition. My attention started shifting more towards the wrong crowd of people.

I came back from summer break more fit and had clear skin and a new hairstyle. Confidence was in the air. I was still devout and held tightly to my faith. With my physique changes, more boys became attracted to me for obvious reasons, and we are not talking about the good type of boys.

I ended up getting exactly what I wanted... attention. Be careful what you wish for! From my lack of self-worth, I fell for the attention I received by guys who could not care less about what I actually was on the inside. I eventually started to find myself in dilemmas, confusion, and temptation. "Should I talk to him?" "No, I don't think it will go well." "I'm going to do it either way." I mean, who else has been in this type of situation? We literally lead ourselves right into it. The more I entertained this, the more my body was alerting me to stop. I tried to ignore and push away all of my anxious feelings, but they never went away. My intuition was clearly telling me that this is what I should not have been doing.

It came to the point when I constantly was asking myself, "how far is too far?" That deeply rooted need for attention started becoming very clear. I didn't even realize it at the time, but it was coming from the lack of emotional presence and guidance from my parents. Physical presence is great, but it also needs to go further than that. Now, this isn't to point fingers or to criticize one's parenting, it is to simply tell the underlying truth. My parents did the best they could at the time, and I love them nonetheless. They are without a doubt the most important people in my life.

There is an important lesson to learn here, and that is the significance of parenting. Like I said before, it will continue to play out as a child develops and becomes into an adult. Some of the things I learned as a kid was that it wasn't good to be vulnerable because it resulted in me being reprimanded, blamed, and lectured. I learned that any show of emotions was because I was overreacting and creating a "Jerry Springer show" scene in my head.

I got told I looked "average" or "okay" on days I felt like I looked beautiful. When I dropped the activities I hated doing and found something (fitness) that I was extremely passionate about, I was told I would quit it "like I quit everything." I do not think that the intention was to make me feel inferior or 'not worthy,' but it sure made me feel that way.

Fathers need to tell and show their daughters how much they are loved and how precious they are. They need to be like a knight in shining armor at all times. They need to protect. They need to care. They need to be emotionally present. They need to be supportive. They need to act on their words. They need to tell us how beautiful we are. They need to tell us and show us the type of man we deserve by being the best father figure. They need to be our greatest teacher and support system; they *should* be this.

But you know what? That's okay. I became stronger and have renounced all of the lies I was told and felt. It made me more understanding, loving, empathetic and compassionate. I was so blessed to change my perception and instead of using all that negativity to create even more negativity. I transmuted it into hard work, optimism, and love. It shaped me to who I am now, and I am forever grateful for it. On top of that, my dad and I have a great relationship today. I love and accept my parents for who they were and who they are.

Anyway, back to sophomore year. My self-worth was so deficient that I let people walk all over me. There were too many times when my inner self didn't want to do something, but I kept telling myself "it's okay, it isn't that big of a deal." So, I basically subconsciously told myself that I didn't care about my body nor my feelings. If I had extreme self-respect, none of these things would've happened. It is extremely important to be aware of this now, so it doesn't lead to more mistakes in the future.

What came to my surprise was that whatever level of self-worth you have, you will get treated accordingly. The result from that shows with the people we attract in our lives. If we attract not the best type of men, then maybe there needs to be some reflection done about who we are and what self-values we possess.

Near the end of the school year, I noticed some of my classmates getting involved in partying, which I had yet to participate in. I began longing to go to parties and be a part of that world. I saw the drama, fun, freedom and attention they were having and getting, and I wanted that. I liked the feeling of getting invited somewhere because it made me feel like I belonged to something. Whether it was with my classmates, on my soccer team, or basically any activity I participated in, I felt excluded most of the time. I was always one of the last people that got picked whenever we played a game. Nobody seemed to want *me*, which is why I craved the feeling of being important. And yet again, I got exactly what I wished for. Cheers to junior year!

Junior Year

The school I attended the first two years of high school closed down due to the lack of funding from our Diocese. The school that originally turned me down accepted my transfer request, which I was thrilled about. I was upset that I would be losing some of my close friends and the unique environment I was in, but at the same time I was more excited to be surrounded by bigger and better opportunities.

My junior year was highlighted by partying, boys and powerlifting.

I got invited to my very first party, but it was more of a get together and only had about 15 people. When I first arrived, I remember thinking that it really was not the most entertaining scene ever. I mean…there was just a group of people sitting together, smoking and drinking. It was somewhat amusing to me, I guess because it was my first time experiencing anything like it. A group of people...sitting together...*just* smoking weed and drinking beer. *Just* doing that. It seemed off to me, it seemed shallow.

There was a girl that arrived later who I have seen on social media that was known for her party life. I immediately noticed who she was, so I made an effort to talk to her. I had no idea that one night would lead to an entire phase of going out almost every weekend.

My first legit party was in October of 2016, and I remember getting there a little early to help out and get to know the girls more. I knew that I had to put more effort in, since I was the "newbie" and had to make my name known. Most of the girls had long falsies (fake eyelashes), even longer nails and glittery eyeshadow, and I thought they looked amazing. It was definitely a look I tried to rock, but I didn't know that you actually had to cut the ends of the falsies off so they would fit your eye shape. It took some time and some pain (the lashes kept poking my eye) until I realized I was doing something wrong. In terms of the whole smoking and drinking aspect, I turned down most of the offers I got in the beginning.

The party began, and since I didn't really have a clique I belonged to yet, I had to "tag" along with people, which is something I strongly disliked doing. It caused me to try too hard when I wanted to be my natural self. To sum up the night, I was trying not to be a misfit, saw some guys I used to associate with, and got alcohol intentionally spilled on my leggings. Wohoo, fun. I went home shortly after that. It wasn't the most successful night, but I knew I was a step closer in getting the life I wanted, or at least thought I wanted.

In terms of my new school and being the new girl, I certainly stood out for the first couple of months. I didn't make a tight circle of friends, but I did have some girls I stuck with for the purpose of having someone to hang out with. Honestly, making friends with girls was hard! They're usually already in cliques, and they aren't too inviting either.

We had an upcoming back-to-school night dance and I was *ready*. I surely made a name for myself that night, and unfortunately, the Dean of students ended up knowing it too. The Dean pulled me out of the dance before it was over and yelled at me for not respecting myself and not knowing any better by inappropriately dancing. To no surprise, I got a Saturday detention. It feels a tad bit weird sharing this in a book, but it was even weirder when my parents got an email from the Dean telling them what happened. The execution of the whole talk could have been better, but he had a point though. I blocked my mind from awareness and tried to justify my behavior as "just having fun." I was starting to lose touch with that innocence that came from my inner self.

At this point, you may ask where my faith went. I put it on the back burner because of the shame I had doing the things I did. It was like a little "break." I will talk more about this in a later chapter.

Despite the punishments from my school and the criticism from my parents, I still felt somewhat good, because I was getting that silly attention I deeply desired. I felt wanted. Looking back at it now, do I even know the girl I am describing? She's much different, but of course I know her. That girl was trying to do her best and simultaneously attempt to fill a void in her heart.

Back to the party phase. I went out for many weekends, and I didn't go out with the best of influences, obviously. Let me paint a picture for you, because some readers might assume I was a crazy party animal. It wasn't really like that. I never did any drugs (other than drinking alcohol, however I stayed around my limit most of the time) because I would see how much of an effect it had on people, and I also didn't want to lose any progress I made at the gym either. My party friends weren't pushy, so whenever I would decline something, they would understand. It's important to be very careful and aware of what is going on at all times, whether it's for yourself or for your friends. Please make sure to hold yourself accountable, you don't have to turn into a wild animal once you step foot into a party nor do you have to participate in a competition based on how many shots you can survive. Have balance.

Honestly, the more I went out, the more I became bored and unsatisfied. It was starting to become apparent that this wasn't the crowd I wanted to hang around and associate myself with. Around the middle of my second semester was when I stopped going out as much and started to focus more on myself. The party scene started becoming "stupid" to me due to a couple of reasons. More significantly, I was tired of it feeling like a waste of time, so I knew I had to change something up. One thing that I should've mentioned is that most of these kickbacks or parties were somewhat "trashy," for lack of a better word. The other thing is how one-dimensional the whole party scene was to me. If you really think about it, it's just a place that's usually overpopulated by guys and almost everyone (if not everyone) is intoxicating their bodies with various forms of drugs. Some become animals and lose their morals. Some do it to escape their reality and pain. Some just become more social. And of course, you can't forget...most are there just because it's "fun." Nothing noteworthy or fulfilling ever comes out of these places, but maybe that's exactly what some people want.

That's just how I see it. Everyone's perception is going to be different along with how they define their "fun" to be.

I feel like I lived a completely different life outside of school and family time. I had different friends, different moral standards, and different behaviors. It was almost like I was living in different worlds. I believed that this partying was something I needed to do most if not every weekend night, to classify myself as "cool" or a part of the popular crowd.

Another way of describing junior year was experiencing (or abusing) the freedom I had. I inherited my mom's car, which allowed me to go anywhere I really wanted to. I loved it. However, just because one has freedom does not excuse them from having responsibilities, and I don't mean that in a "you must do your chores!!" kind of way. First and foremost, you are responsible for yourself, including your well-being, happiness, and mental health.

Aside from working out for two to three hours, five to six times a week, I dishonored my mind, body and soul. I completely left God because I was ashamed of my lifestyle. I was a doormat to boys, and I constantly went against my intuition, which always resulted in many internal conflicts.

Thankfully, this phase died out near the end of my junior year, mainly because I got a boyfriend. I thought I was in deep doo-doo already, but I had no idea what was coming.

Senior Year

It was my last year of high school. All of the students, including me, knew that we really had to grind out the first semester for the sake of perfect report cards for college. I really tried making an effort to put my heart into the things that mattered most to me, but I was constantly in a battle that held me back with everything I did. It isn't possible to thrive and grow when you're carrying a massive garbage bag. And what was in that garbage bag? My relationship.

As expected, my lack of self-worth caught up to me like the plague, and it showed from the extremely toxic relationship I was in. In the very beginning, things felt off on my end. I had so much anxiety that I tried drowning it out, and of course, it never worked. I seriously thought there was something wrong with me. "Why was I so anxious?" Knowing now, it was that intuition and gut feeling in me that was screaming to be heard, but my lack of awareness and recklessness wanted nothing to do with it.

You know what's funny? I convinced myself that this guy was better than the other guys I talked to simply because I got an ounce more of respect and attention. Self-worth? Yeah, we didn't know her back then. Like I said, I had no idea what was coming. Let's keep going.

There wasn't really a "honeymoon phase" that I hear many couples go through, so it all started out messy. Just a couple of months into the relationship, the emotional rollercoasters began. Just envision your typical immature and toxic high school relationship because… it was exactly that. Have you girls ever had to beg your boyfriends to celebrate monthly dating anniversaries? Right, well that was just one of the "things."

Ironically, the more arguments we would have, the closer I would emotionally feel to him. Isn't that crazy? My feelings would get tied up even more, and so it began harder to leave and abandon him for good. Chance after chance, I forgave and hoped for some change. I constantly questioned how a person could be so oblivious to hurting someone's feelings that they claimed to love and then shed alligator tears when they wanted to end things. It made absolutely no sense to me, but then again, I had hope. And with me clinging onto that hope, I slowly but surely began to lose myself in the process. I let the many cons outweigh the small list of pros.

"Please never ever call me that word again."

"Why did I find a picture of another girl on your phone?"

"Why did you change your password?"

"Why are you constantly bringing up my past?"

"Why wouldn't you post me on your Instagram?"

"Why would you call me a psycho just because I wanted someone to take a picture of us?"

"Why can't I meet your mom?"

"Why do you value going to a party over hanging out with me?"

Me: But don't worry Nastassia, if he says he loves you then he loves you. Maybe the love will one day change the way he treats you.

I received more red flags than red rose petals on a bouquet. There were more tears than happy memories. I was lost, hurt, and stuck.

Obviously, because of how emotionally caught up and drained I was in the relationship, I didn't focus enough on myself, school, family and dreams. I would've never thought how emotionally draining a relationship like this could really be until I was actually in one. I went through eight months of tears, anxiety, verbal abuse and personal stagnation. It turned into a constant battle between trying to win my boyfriend's attention and time which resulted in a broken dynamic. I even began to become controlling because I was against him doing most of the things he did and the way he behaved. And the very simple things I expected him to do were not met one single bit.

I was not aware at the time that this was not right of me to do. I settled into the relationship and then expected change to happen with things I personally did not approve of. Recipe for disaster, but a key lesson was learned here.

You cannot try to change people who are not conscious of their own behavior, so do not bother at all. Let go in peace and strive to connect with people who share the same values, morals, and behaviors as you have.

Almost all of the arguments and breakups resulted in the classic "okay, I promise I will be different," which I fell for. Every…Single…Time. Goodness gracious, it's like I became a doormat all of a sudden! Anyway, you get the drift. Let's turn the tables around.

A couple of months into 2018, something happened that filled me with fear, so I wanted to go to the police station to see if any safety measures could be taken. I was in a vulnerable state, and of course I wanted my boyfriend to support and comfort me by going with me. I wanted him to be my knight in shining armor.

Funny joke.

Long story short, an argument arose due to him misinterpreting something I said, so he ended up bailing which was the last straw for me. Any feelings and tolerance I had remaining were wiped out, and this time around things were different. I never became so mad before, and I actually felt *done.*

"How could you do that?

"I really *needed* you, I asked you to do one simple thing for me, and you flaked on me?"

Even with the same manipulation and the fake promises, there was no bone in my body that wanted to go back to that. I knew that it was all bullsh*t anyway. It took me about a thousand trials, but hey, I finally got there and began realizing all of the nonsense I was put through.

Two weeks after that, I found out some really unexpected news, and to say I was surprised would be an understatement. When you hear the words, "he isn't who you think he is," your automatic reaction is disbelief.

Was it a joke?

Did it really happen?

But he told me he would never do that?

How long ago did this happen?

Who was involved?

Are you sure…?

It did happen, and it hit me like a train.

The shock numbed my body, anxiety made me cold, nausea commenced, and I felt like I was in a whole different world. It was undeniably the worst feeling I have ever experienced, and what made it even worse was that I couldn't do that much about it except wait it out. When nighttime came, it was just me, my anxiety, and the anticipation for the end of what felt like hell. Not to mention, I was angry and wanted revenge, another feeling I never had before.

Another thought that was racing through my mind was that he had no idea who he just messed with…

Two days later, I confronted him about the cheating, and to no surprise, I got lied to. That same night I was paralyzed with anxiety and had to skip school because I ran on a couple of hours of sleep and knew that I would not be able to focus on anything. Throughout all of these negative emotions, I simultaneously knew that I was nearing the end of the storm and the beginning of a beautiful and long-lasting rainbow; I felt liberated for the first time in a long time. And that, my friends, is exactly what happened.

Regardless of all that, I am immensely grateful that it happened to me because it changed my entire life around. As crazy as it may seem, it was a blessing in disguise. It was the exact catalyst I needed for my transformation that was so profound and powerful for me. You will get to see it for yourself very soon.

Let's go back to school. My entire college application and acceptance process wasn't too important to me. I never had a "dream" school, nor did I really resonate with all of the majors offered. When the time for college applications came, I applied to four UC's, two state colleges and one overpriced Catholic university. I considered myself to be a solid student as well, but I guess other colleges didn't see that. I ended up getting rejected by all of the UC's and only getting accepted into two colleges.

I definitely did some things in senior year that I wasn't too proud of. Certain classes I cheated in, even on the SATs, all so that I wouldn't make my parents disappointed which I felt like I was doing often. I mean, I really did despise taking standardized tests and naturally did poorly on them.

On top of that, I felt like I needed to compete with my classmates who seemed to be much smarter than I was. My school praised the students that had the best grades and were the best in their sport, which is understandable, but how about everyone else? One size doesn't fit all, and this is where school fails us. I can spend hours talking about how broken our system is, so I will only bring up some of my opinions while we are on it.

- I think it is absolutely ridiculous to be required to take x amount of years on certain types of subjects to fulfill high school requirements. Calculus? Chemistry? History? Ask yourself, how many times have you used these subjects in the real world? "Oh, but people should know about this material anyway." It's brain filling material unless actually used later down the road. Don't forget, *all* information is accessible through the power of the internet. If a person has no desire or future relevance of applying these topics in their lives, why would she or he be required to take it?

- Simply put, the results of our grades reflect how well we can memorize material. Why would I need to memorize Physics formulas I will never again use in my life if I can find it online within seconds?

- The education system does not prep anyone for adulthood. Taxes? Success? Emotional intelligence? Overcoming fears? Mental health? Investing? Financial education? Confidence building vs. insecurity and ego?

- It values the kids with the perfect report cards and involvement much more and makes students who don't do that feel inferior. Many of the most successful people in the world had little to no education, and most didn't even graduate from college. This clearly is an indicator.

How can I be innovative and creative when I am constantly bombarded and confined by the next "required" class, test, or homework?

Of course, there will be people who argue that even though these subjects may not be later applied to life, they will make you develop important brain solving abilities. I mean, sure...if you would rather waste your time learning irrelevant and trivial topics instead of actually practicing and improving in what you are really passionate about, then by all means, continue doing what you do.

Knowledge is not power. Knowledge is *potential* power. If it isn't used, it's pretty much useless.

My dad introduced me to another great entrepreneur, thinker, and philanthropist named Naval Ravikant. He is known for creating a company named AngelList which is for startups, angel investors, and jobseekers looking to work at startups. I was looking more into him and found him speak about specific knowledge, something that Napoleon Hill dedicated a chapter of his book, *Think and Grow Rich* to. Naval said, "The first thing to notice about specific knowledge is that you can't be trained for it. If you can be trained for it, if you can go to a class and learn specific knowledge, then somebody else can be trained for it too, and then we can mass-produce and mass-train people. Heck, we can even program computers to do it and eventually we can program robots to walk around doing it. So, if that's the case, then you're extremely replaceable and all we have to pay you is the minimum wage that we have to pay you to get you to do it when there are lots of other takers who can be trained to do it."

Nothing much else for me to say since he said it quite well.

Let me give you a relevant example. I love being an entrepreneur and have possessed entrepreneur-like qualities since middle school. There is absolutely no better way for me to test my brain capabilities than to actually start a business and try to expand it instead of sitting in a classroom listening to someone teach me about it who might not even practice what he or she preaches or even believe the class is necessary to be a successful entrepreneur. It's like learning about working out, how many sets/reps to do, and what the best exercises are but never doing the actual workout. Does that seem logical to you?

There are many parents, including my own, who have told me about this so-called important brain training that comes through subjects like these, but the best "brain training" you will get is learning how to use your brain for yourself instead of letting other people influence how you think. Period.

I only applied to the UC's because my ego told me it would boost up my reputation and please my family. A lot of unconscious ego was in me at the time, creating not the best of intentions.

Quick story. I was the worst student out of a little over a dozen students in my Spanish 4 class, and my teacher didn't help with my already fragile self-esteem knowing I was surrounded by some of the smartest kids in school. I already knew that my Spanish vocabulary and speaking skills were far behind the rest of my classmates, yet I still continued on with the class.

I remember we had an upcoming quiz that I probably spent five minutes or less studying in my car for, and when we got the results back, I received a failing grade. Not a shocker. My teacher then came up to me and asked if I had a "mental blockage" when taking the quiz. No Señora, I did not have a mental blockage, I just did not care enough to study. I would never say that, but I found it to be an interesting word choice. It definitely gave me the vibe that she thought I was completely inadequate.

That's another common shortcoming of school system's; it's easier for teachers to judge students and critique them for failing instead of trying to understand why they got the grade they did. In my case, I didn't spend enough time studying because I simply didn't care, but to assume that there was something that failed mentally in my head while taking the quiz was not the best approach.

My favorite person ever, Gary Vaynerchuk (who I love and adore and know that one day I will meet through the power of manifestation and hard work), talks about this all the time. He is a great example of a person who did not do well in school and had some of his teachers condemn him for that. He questioned the teachers who judged him if they were happy with their jobs, which usually resulted in them ignoring that question. Not a shocker. Gary turned out to be doing just fine, making hundreds of millions of dollars through his businesses and influencing millions of people around the world, including me.

Do not get me wrong. School can be beneficial depending on what you want to study and do. I did well in subjects I was actually interested in like Economics, AP English Language (I had a wonderful teacher), Environmental Ethics, Social Ethics and Justice, and Philosophy of Religion. I really enjoyed learning about philosophy, religion, and gaining awareness of what's going on in our environment. I am actually extremely fortunate to have learned the things I learned.

What I am getting at is that not everyone wants to be a star student because some people aren't called to be that, or they understand that grades aren't as meaningful as people in the school and the education system makes it out to be. Being educated is extremely necessary in order to thrive, but there is also a harsh line that needs to be drawn between useful education and simply "brain filling" education.

The grade system is not the real world. However, I can agree that it does show some level of discipline and great memorization and thinking abilities. I am not trying to diss school in any way, I am simply trying to shed light on how our schools do not prepare us for the real world and teach us how to be successful. We are only taught how to acquire jobs, and yet some people don't even get that after they have received their college degrees. I personally see this as a robotic routine: finish high school, get a college degree, get a job, and then get married. Although this is the well-known traditional route, I am very happy to see it disintegrate very slowly as more people are starting to realize that being schooled doesn't equate to success.

That was my little talk on high school and college. All in all, my senior year was an emotional rollercoaster. Next!

Chapter 4

Knowing Your Worth

"If someone is not treating you with love and respect, it is a gift if they walk away from you. If that person doesn't walk away, you will surely endure many years of suffering with him or her. Walking away may hurt for a while, but your heart will eventually heal..."
--Don Miguel Ruiz

The definition of self-worth is, "the opinion you have about yourself and the value you place on yourself." This is so incredibly important, and it isn't solely applicable to women. It is equally as important for men. Self-love, self-esteem, or whatever you want to call it, it was definitely a massive struggle for me and is something that so many people struggle with as well. If some of us truly possessed this value for ourselves, then we wouldn't make so many mistakes nor deal with them.

I will repeat this many times throughout the book. The way we grow up emotionally and mentally is predicated by a couple of things: how our parents raised us, whether our parents were present emotionally and physically, and how the entire family dynamic is. Questions like these all come into play. Are your parents divorced or do they have a stable and healthy marriage? Did your parents give you love and nurture? Did your dad leave? Were your parent's great role models or became examples of how not to act?

We emulate our parents. So, if the environment (family dynamic) is loud, abusive, and chaotic, then most likely that will reappear in the child and their future. Just an example. One of my favorite authors, Don Miguel Ruiz, talks about "domestication" many times in his books. He starts with saying our first domesticators are our parents, whether it be good or bad. The people we begin to learn from at a very early age influence us greatly; we see what they do, how they do it, their reactions and then we start to believe these things as the truth and the way of life, which then creates us to emulate those attitudes and behaviors subconsciously. Parenting is of extreme importance and is the foundation of a child's future.

Some time ago, I realized that most parents really don't have it all and even most *people* don't have it all. This became so apparent to me when I gained self-awareness and took a step back to see how other people around me communicated and reacted to certain things. I began noticing what they were saying and the fear behind their words.

I learned that the way people react to anything and anyone is a true reflection of their inner self and the beliefs they have set in their minds. That pride, anger and jealousy was just a mask for insecurity and the different ways the ego presents itself. And finally, I learned that there is a much deeper meaning that is present in a person's behavior. I finally started seeing *the why* and how there is a deeper reasoning to everything a person does, says, and thinks.

One obvious difference between a parent and a child is age. With this means that it is quicker for a child to relearn and change their habits, as opposed to an adult who has certain things ingrained in their heads for a longer amount of time. Just like an addict trying to heal from their addiction, it is difficult for an adult to try to break from their habits and traditional values. Unfortunately, many adults never work on their insecurities, fears and traumas, and therefore all of it gets thrown onto the child, but the child is not yet aware of why that's happening in the first place.

This is what happened to me. I did not understand why certain things were said to me, so it was much harder for me to forgive everything they did and said that hurt me. On top of that, it made me a little bit resentful. When I started reading a lot of books, it came to my attention that all of this had very little to do with me, and more on the way they were on the inside. I understood and felt empathetic to it. I forgave internally because I knew that they didn't mean it. Deep down inside there is love, goodness, and innocence in everyone.

The most common consequence of having the lack of self-worth that I have experienced and seen many others do is settling. Setting the bar way too low for what they actually deserve, both girls and boys. Or the set standards become neglected because we all know that when feelings get involved, it is a different playing field.

To settle for someone essentially means to let go of the aspects of that person that don't fit your standards, morals, beliefs, and other things that are important to you. You begin to "compromise" for many reasons. You may want to feel loved, get attention, avoid being lonely, or you may feel comfortable with that person and you don't want to disappoint him or her. If those are the cases, then chances are you won't even feel *right* or *good* with fully committing yourself, which will not only waste your time, but the other person's as well.

The people we associate ourselves with typically reflects our level of self-worth. You want to make the other person a better him/her, and you would want to have that reciprocated, I would hope so. The recipient can't really do that if they are not in your league mentally, intellectually, spiritually, and anything else that applies. If you are religious or spiritual, it wouldn't be good to settle for someone who is not. Another crucial piece we should be aware of is the long-term. Yeah, maybe for now we feel in love and on Cloud 9, but how about in the future? For example, I see a lot of women going to Mass with their kids, but no father is present. That may be for many reasons, but I know for sure that some of the fathers don't go because they don't share the same beliefs.

For me, I need someone who is a direct reflection of myself or ideally better. Oh, I know that somebody like that is not waiting around the corner, but I would rather be single and wait for him even if it takes years than settle and compromise my standards. I can fall in love with a stranger if I really wanted to, but I need to know what you can bring to the table and if you can bring it consistently.

Self-worth is the ability to say "no" to something that you know isn't good for you and won't bring you closer to your goals or to becoming a better person. Now that is something we should aspire to. You should know yourself by now to realize what is good and what is bad for you. I can tell your firsthand, that if you are used to falling into temptation and going back to people or things that serve you no greater purpose, it is quite a challenging process to break out of that habit. It takes constant effort of letting go and disassociating yourself from certain parts of your past until you completely forget about what ever bothered or disturbed you in the first place. It takes time, healing, and working on your inner self so that you become mentally strong and emotionally ready for any challenge that may pop up.

If you want to remove yourself fully from anything that won't help you grow, remove it from your life then. Do whatever it takes, but make sure you do it in a loving manner. When I slowly started getting over my party phase, I started disassociating myself with the people I used to party with. Nothing on them, I just didn't want to be around that crowd nor spend my time on something rather useless for me.

There will be mistakes along the way as well, but it is important to not let them discourage you or make you feel disappointed in yourself. Fail, acknowledge what went wrong and find how you can avoid it next time, get up and go.

Healing in general is a long, yet very fruitful process. It takes a lot of courage to forgive those who did us wrong, as well as to forgive ourselves, but I will talk about the topic of forgiveness a little later. It is that constant state of being "under construction," periods of weeding, digging, rehabilitating and then planting, watering and nurturing, figuratively of course. A beautiful and full blooming garden is only like that because it has been taken care of properly, lovingly and carefully. Once all flowers and plants have bloomed, only then can gardeners cut off the prettiest flowers and give them to someone else. I am sure all of us have heard of the phrase, "you can't love someone if you don't love yourself." I'm saying the same exact thing. You can't just cut off a flower when it hasn't bloomed, there would be no point. Likewise, you cannot love someone or try to be your best to someone if you are in no prime mental and emotionally shape.

Personally, my process of healing from my ex-boyfriend was a rollercoaster. I had times when I questioned if I made any progress at all. I had weeks when I would do really well, and then a bad week would hit me. I was like, "really? All of this work to feel like crap again?" Those low moments eventually became less and less painful up to the point where I now don't experience them anymore.

Patience is key. As long as you keep at it, there's always a light at the end of the tunnel. You might not see it yet, but I guarantee you that if you put the work in every single day, it will appear. Those who say "it never worked" are usually the ones who gave up a little too early before seeing the results.

We need to fully understand that anything good and long-lasting will not come overnight. As I said, it's constantly trying, succeeding, failing and getting up. It makes us strong, it builds our character and it shapes our future. We hear the term "trust the process" thrown around all of the time, but most of us never consistently apply that attitude. When thinking about change, we should be realistically looking at months and years. The sooner we start the closer we will be to achieving greatness!

Chapter 5

Not Good Enough?

*"To realize that you are not your thoughts is when you
begin to awaken spiritually."*
--Eckhart Tolle

Loving yourself isn't easy, especially when you are
your own worst critic! It's quite difficult because there are
so many expectations whether it is coming from our
family, society, friends or all of the above. I was always told
and felt that I wasn't good enough, smart enough nor
beautiful enough. Not good enough for who? Not smart
enough for who? Not beautiful enough for who? Through
which check list did someone analyze me through and
decide all of this from?

Let me start off by saying that it isn't true. We live in
a world where rules, opinions, and judgements can be
made by anyone at any time. Additionally, most people say
things and make decisions based off of their feelings, which
could change at any second. Let's imagine a man who is
full of love. He wants to share and spread that love with
everyone around him because he has so much of it that it

overflows onto other people. This is what naturally happens. We have one end of that spectrum, so let's dive to the other end. Now, let's imagine a woman who is so unhappy and unsatisfied with herself that she wants to project her unhappiness with everyone else around her. She has a very low amount of love in herself and doesn't think she is good enough, and therefore she judges other people based on that lack of satisfaction within herself. This is yet another natural reaction. Most people tend to fall in the middle of that spectrum.

Basically, what I am trying to say is that any judgement someone makes is based on a reflection of themselves. This is *exactly* why we shouldn't take any negativity seriously. Quite frankly, we shouldn't even take praise seriously. Our worth shouldn't come from neither of these two opposites because it needs to come from within. For example, let's take a model who bases her worth off of her known beauty that gets massive amounts of reciprocation from her social media followers. Imagine that one day, she gains a couple of pounds and her followers begin to notice it. Then, they start calling her fat, obese, and overweight even if she really isn't. As a result, she begins hating herself and resenting her body because she has matched her identity and worth into the praise she was receiving. It's a recipe for disaster to base your worth by the way other people perceive you. What matters is how *you* perceive yourself.

It takes time, work and reflection to heal from the lies we were told. We also need to have a certain level of awareness to not even let these comments affect us in the first place. Like I said, it is a direct reflection of the commentator, not you. So, of course I was good enough! Of course, I was smart enough! I didn't have to be a 4.0 student and be on top of my education to know that I would turn out just fine. My type of "smart" didn't satisfy the path that my parents wanted me to go down, and that was totally okay. I believe that nobody should sacrifice who they are and what they want to do for the sake of making someone else happy, it just isn't fair. We only have one beautiful and precious life, one mind and one body. If we are constantly thinking of pleasing mom and dad or whoever else, well then we will ultimately let ourselves down. And whose thoughts are you listening to right before you got to bed? Yours. I know how much some of us hate those negative nightly thoughts. We need to change that around. Do not hinder your potential for success and a happier life. This means not succumbing to the lies and opinions of others. As long as you truly know yourself, that is the only person you need to listen to.

As discussed earlier, parents play the biggest role in a child's life. If they want to have a successful relationship with their children, then they must guide and support them into becoming their best and happiest selves.

I believe it is very unreasonable for a parent to think of a child as a disgrace or "not good enough" because he or she ended up having a different profession, sexuality, ideal, or attitude than what that parent envisioned them to have. It isn't fair to press ideals because it will just cause so much resentment. Many people including me have dealt with this, and we know how unfortunate it is when our parents don't align with our desires. All children want the same thing from their parents, and that's to be deeply loved and supported.

I am coming from a place of deep passion when I say you only have *one* life. You can choose to either make it a good one or a bad one. You can either love yourself or loathe yourself, live a meaningful life or a meaningless one. And trust me, enjoying life and making it meaningful is so worth it. It's what we are meant to do. God didn't intend to put us here on Earth so we can make our lives a living hell. It really is up to you and the mindset you choose to take. Wouldn't it be such a relief to wake up feeling genuinely joyful to start your day knowing how blessed you are?

This may be a hard pill to swallow for some, but it is important to know that every little self-doubt, insecurity, and fear we have is all created in our minds. All of the events that happened to us are from the past and will remain in the past, unless we purposefully choose not to let go of them. When I first learned this, it made me play

So...

the victim role a little bit. It was more like "you are telling me that all of the awful things I went through are basically irrelevant and that I should feel nothing about them?" "But this person did x, y and z to me! I can't get over that." The honest answer that I have come to realize myself is yes and no. Yes, what happened to many of us has been unjust, undeserved, and heartbreaking. At the same time, everything we experienced in the past doesn't have to be part of our present. This isn't being insensitive; it's being realistic and moving on for the sake of our well-being. It's hard to come to that destination, but it is also very freeing when you get there. Forgiveness is the main component to moving on, and it is something I will be talking about soon.

Bottom line is that I am good enough. You are good enough. We are good enough. We need to start accepting and loving ourselves for who we are. We don't need to cover up and hide. Whose opinions are you listening to? Whose judgements are you becoming insecure from?

One of the most liberating feelings is to come to terms with the fact that the person who is doing the judging, criticizing, or naysaying carries a level of truth that reflects himself or herself through their thoughts and words. Throughout my entire life, I have been told I couldn't accomplish what I wanted to be and do, but that's only because the people who said that have given up on their own dreams and desires. It's simple. Oprah said, "Self-esteem comes from being able to define the world in your own terms and refusing to abide by the judgments of others." Amen.

Accept your intrinsic goodness because you *are* good. Look at yourself in the mirror and say that. Say that whenever you are showering, praying, or meditating. Say it on your car ride home. Say it and feel it. It's powerful. You can change your exterior in whatever way you want, but your interior is what takes real work, and this is something that no money nor cardio machine can change. You wouldn't even need to change a single thing about your outside if you simply accept yourself from the inside out. It isn't an overnight process because rewiring set beliefs that have grown on us is challenging. But if you start right now, future you is going to be so grateful.

Let's talk a little more about self-love. I saw Jay Shetty post something quite significant on his Instagram that's worth sharing. The post said, "if YOU treat yourself well, you won't let anyone treat you badly. If YOU treat yourself badly, you won't let anyone treat you well." This describes self-love accurately. If I had the amount of self-love I have now, I wouldn't bother to associate myself with men who wanted me for superficial reasons, I wouldn't let myself down like that. Having a lack of self-worth creates us to settle and get ourselves into situations we don't *really* want to be in.

I believe our worth comes from what our parents instilled in us. For example, we've all heard the word "daddy issues" used on a woman who might've had instability issues with other men or acted a certain way to be called that. The term actually rings a lot of truth to it knowing of the significant impact having a present, affectionate and loving father (and both parents in general) makes. It makes all of the difference in the world, for both men and women.

The reasoning is plain and simple, when girls or women seek attention and validation from boys, it is usually the result of either a broken bond or something vital missing between father and daughter. This disconnection may exist from emotional or physical absence, verbal or physical abuse, or any other issues that created trauma whether it was conscious or subconscious.

I recently had a great talk with a wonderful priest named Fr. Justin. We talked about my High School years because I was still unclear why I acted the way I did. Yes, it was from the lack of self-love and respect, but it has to go deeper than that. Fr. Justin said that with every feeling and action, there is a deep desire rooted in it that intrinsically points to something holy. I couldn't find that desire for the life of me, I don't think I was *really* looking for anything in the way that some people seek to be validated or loved from other men. I think it might've been sheer curiosity about boys and relationships. After 30 minutes of listening to me and asking questions, he came up with the assumption that I was very good at blocking out emotions. I had that "aha" moment...yes, I really was good at doing that back then. I went further and asked myself "why?" The answer came quickly. My entire life my parents told me that my emotions were invalid, that I was making stuff up in my head, and that I was always overdramatic.

If you remember what I put in my High School chapters, I told you I had a lot of anxiety doing the things I did. I also said that every single time my heart would tell me to stop, I would ignore it. I tried blocking out my feelings. My curiosity led me to plunge deep into all of the wrong places even though I received all of the "no's" in the world from my body.

Think of self-love as a spiritual seed that is planted inside of us that grows and grows until it eventually starts touching things outside of us. Other people, to be exact. When we have love within ourselves, it shows, because we love everything and everybody around us. We do not see people, and then judge them because we see them for their intrinsic worth, which every single human being has. Another term for this is "seeing in the eyes of love," it is not easy, and it is something that I try to do every day. Jesus is the most perfect example of this. Even in the midst of immense suffering and betrayal, He gives praise to His Father and forgives people for all of their wrongdoings by saying "Father, forgive them, for they do not know what they are doing" (Luke 23:34). Even with those who have wronged Him the most, He continued to forgive and love. He died for humanity out of love for love...that's powerful.

The thing is, all of us want love. Some of us might not go in the right route to attain it, but this is still that deep-rooted desire Fr. Justin spoke about. We want to give love and have it be reciprocated, which is hereditary because we were all made with this. In John 4:17, it is written that, "And so we know and rely on the love God has for us. God is love. Whoever lives in love lives in God, and God in him." If we add in Genesis 1:27, "God said, "Let Us make man in Our image, after Our likeness," then it is our proof that we are certainly made with love and in love. It is an innate desire in us that will *never* go away.

Unfortunately, it becomes a problem when people focus their time loving and giving attention to others instead of doing the same for themselves. We may even misuse love for our own personal benefit, begin using other people or get used, maybe we seek out that lost connection in wrong ways such as lust, sex or pornography, and essentially using any distraction we can instead of solving the problem. It becomes more of seeing in the eyes of *"what can I get from you"* instead of *"how can I love you purely for who you are."* We begin viewing others as objects used for our own personal and selfish benefit. There is no way that interpersonal relationship can be made, which should be the goal with the people we interact with. I often recommend for a person to work on themselves first before settling into something else. I actually *highly* encourage to grow in self-love before trying to love someone.

We see it a lot. Girl and boy get together. Boy (or girl, but I will use boy in this case) grew up in a broken home so boy ultimately seeks love by dating other people thinking this is what he needs and that it will fill the void in his heart. Girl and boy have fun, they fall in love with each other. Gradually, boy begins to show negative signs. He no longer begins treating girl the way he originally did when he courted her. Boy uncovers more and more of his unsolved emotional baggage onto the relationship. Girl gets sad and feels unloved. The relationship becomes toxic. Both boy and girl become so hurt and they break things off for good.

It's a classic story we have all been in or have experienced someone go through. The cause comes from never properly healing and having a false perception that a new relationship will solve the original problems. It never does.

This is something that I have to say due to me being extremely empathetic and compassionate towards girls. Ladies, if you feel inclined to stay in a toxic relationship because you think you can't get anyone "better," you are gravely mistaken. And if you think that he will magically change his abusive ways and begin treating you with the respect you deserve, you are also mistaken. Love sometimes can blind us from seeing that person's true colors.

You are worthy. You are loved. You do deserve better, you deserve all of the goodness this world has. You are perfect. Sister, you are made for love. Good, pure and genuine love.

Same thing with men. You are a King and deserve to find the perfect Queen for you. Perfection, however, doesn't come from how they look. There are millions of girls who are beautiful, but what really matters is the beauty they hold within their soul.

"Love is patient, love is kind. It does not envy, it does not boast, it is not proud. It does not dishonor others, it is not self-seeking, it is not easily angered, it keeps no record of wrongs. Love does not delight in evil but rejoices with the truth. It always protects, always trusts, always hopes, always perseveres" (Corinthians 13:4-7). I started tearing up in Mass when I heard this being used as one of the readings. This quote from the Bible really resonated with me at the time through its truth, power and beauty. Love IS all of that, and all of us deserve it! Love is not toxic, love does not make you cry. Love most certainly does not make you question why you do not seem good enough. Love is beautiful, uplifting, peacemaking and reassuring.

For some of us, practicing self-love can include breaking old habits and toxic behaviors. We could let go of people who we know aren't meant to be in our lives. It can be to stop the self-harm or looking in the mirror and being unhappy with who you see. It can be to improve the health of our bodies by running or working out, trying to pray and meditate, seeing food as a positive instead of a negative, doing anything that brings you peace, buying yourself flowers, and just overall nurturing yourself. Oh, and you can't forget, practicing forgiveness.

Majority of people are overstimulated by what's inside their social media, their relationships, and their drama that they run out of time to take care of themselves. So many of us never prioritize what's truly important because either we are so concerned with outwardly happenings and/or we don't think we deserve to love ourselves.

At first, you can take baby steps. 15 minutes before you go to bed, read a book. Say "thank you" when you wake up that God blessed you with another day. Go for a little hike on a weekend. Put your phone on airplane mode, you deserve to give yourself that break. Take time to be mindful of your breath throughout the day. These are all things we can *easily* incorporate in our lives. Our day to day lives will significantly change for the better with these little additions.

Not Good Enough?

Sometimes, our minds are filled with so many distorted expectations from our environment, society, parents and/or friends. We start to base our lives and our values off of something someone said, something that's popular or something that is based on tradition. When we don't attain what we want or think we want, we criticize ourselves. Many of us may also strive for perfection but always fall short because that type of perfection is subjective. It isn't the truth, it is only our perception that was formed through what people told us looked better and what looked worse, what was popular and what wasn't popular. The only real perfection that exists is simply YOU. You are perfect because you were made in the image and likeness of God. You are a reflection of His work. That is your intrinsic state and this Truth can never be changed.

We sometimes spend way too much time nit-picking every little thing about ourselves, further creating insecurities that can lead to depression, anxiety, resentment, and hatred. So then by the time we try to work on ourselves, we have all of these things we need to battle! We lack so much awareness that we continue to waste our time trying so hard to be perfect superficially. So much time is wasted when it could've been spent on something productive and life changing.

When I actually started gripping the reins of my life, I started to become peaceful, aware, happy, and an overall more authentic person. Everything in my life elevated. I began focusing on overcoming anything that challenged me, especially mentally. I launched my first business called Nasty Fit and am currently working on a very exciting and fulfilling business that will launch in 2020. I have also started growing a team around me and taking the necessary steps to create an actually sustainable business. Overall, I am constantly creating my most successful self. What point am I trying to get at? Growing in self-love creates a domino effect. You begin to open you mind to new ideas, creativity, love, and greatness and influence others to do the same as well.

Chapter 6

The Four Bodies

"You can only lose something that you have, but you cannot lose something that you are."
--Eckhart Tolle

When I read *The Power of No* by Claudio and James Altucher, that's how I first came across this idea which made an insane amount of sense. It was one of those "aha" moments. I believe that in order to become your best self, these four have to be at play all day every day.

By working on improving these, everything will change. Not only will it elevate you, but it will also change the lenses that you use to see the world around with. This idea includes the *emotional body, spiritual body, physical body and mental body*. Let's go over these in depth:

Mental: This is essentially your mindset and perception. Your goals, ideas, and opinions can be found here. If you have a weak mindset, you will most likely not reach your goals and succumb to your doubts, fears and insecurities. If you have a strong mindset, you have overcome those doubts and fears and have taken control of your mind. This is where discipline is built. It is also internal, but it does manifest itself outwardly by how you speak, act and behave (through our emotions). Weak minded people float in life and do not have any set goals and plans; strong-minded people are determined, dedicated, disciplined and have faith in what they want to accomplish and make out of life. I strongly recommend reading *Outwitting the Devil* by Napoleon Hill, his entire book is essentially based on the mind.

Emotional: These are our emotions. Everything and anyone you encounter will influence your emotions, and this will be shown through your reaction and response. It is an external energy because it manifests from our mental body into our emotional body. For example, if someone has an extremely negative outlook on life, they are going to show it. They will get irritated and angry faster as well as be more susceptible to being sad. Someone who is at peace and content with their lives, will manifest that into being happy and loving towards other people in the way that speak, behave and act.

Physical: This is another external body and it is the only body that can be tangible. Physical has everything to do with our bodies and our health. Someone who is fit and healthy will be able to think clearer, feel better, and live an overall better life. Not only that, but the rest of our three bodies actually play a role in this too. If we exercise but still are very broken internally, then that has a high chance that will affect your health in the long run.

Spiritual: The spiritual body brings a wonderful feeling of fulfillment, belonging and security. It is knowing that there is more out there, that there is something in us that can resonate with something Divine and Holy. Our souls long for a spiritual purpose, which is why It does not resonate from the pleasures of the world. To some, it can be a certain religion and to others it can be living a highly spiritual life (both of these are similar in some aspects but overall different). The longing can only be satisfied with the improvement of our spiritual life, our relationship with God. It's the most fulfilling, elevating and gratifying feeling I have ever experienced. I believe that if we master this aspect, we will overall become happier, and more loving and peaceful people.

Be honest with yourself and reflect on what body or bodies are lacking in your life. Once you figure this out, try working on them. If you feel better, then that is a clear sign that this is what you need to focus on.

There was an article I read that said, "each body should be balanced—and make up 25% of our wholeness." Relating this back to my life, my last three years of high school was only comprised of having the physical body on lock. I mean, I went to the gym almost every day, it was my *life.* Mentally, I was somewhat there because I did push myself hard in the things I wanted to do, and through that

I did create some discipline. Still, not even close to where I am today.

The four bodies are to be practiced every single day. It deals with yourself, your interaction with others, and your connection with something bigger than yourself (whether you choose to call that God, the Holy Trinity, Universe, etc.). That is what life is about, and how you go about it will determine whether you walk your path in fulfillment and contentment or depression, regret, and unrest. Now that you know these four and are aware of them, you have no excuse!

Chapter 7

Temptations, Fears and Insecurities

"Our only limitations are the ones we set up in our own minds"
--Napoleon Hill

We have all dealt with temptation, fear, and insecurities. Most of us even experience this on a daily basis. It sometimes stops us from doing something we really want to do because we let it overcome our desires. We need to put an end to that. Yes, you. Look at that quote at the top of the page from Napoleon Hill…it's true. We limit, and limit, and limit ourselves like no other. Then we try to convince ourselves to settle in mediocrity and permanently stay in our comfort zones. Meanwhile, we try to put the blame on everything and everyone around us for this issue so we could feel better about ourselves.

I do not know every single one of your problems, obviously, but I do know that many people face fear, in one way or another. There are many types of it: fear of criticism, change, failing, taking a leap of faith into the unknown, letting go, messing up, trying, and even the fear of success. The insecurities so many of us feed our minds with like being too ugly, too fat, too skinny, too stupid, too tall, too short, too useless, and the one we are all familiar by now, not being good enough. All of these things completely stop us from becoming our most authentic and best selves. They stop us from being happy and at peace with our lives. We start floating away more and more from our core being and purpose.

We were born innocent, pure, carefree, and unstoppable! We always dreamed big when we were kids. What happened to all of that?

Don Miguel Ruiz, a profound and very wise author, calls this process "domestication." According to him, this is "a concept rooted in the Native American Toltec tradition. The elders recognized domestication, a system of behavior control based on reward and punishment, as the biggest obstacle to personal freedom for human beings." That is exactly what it is, "the biggest obstacle to personal freedom." Once we lock up in our minds, we begin locking up in our lives. The cycle repeats itself until we choose to stop it and rewire our minds to think differently. Oh, the power our thoughts have.

This process starts with our parents, who are our first role models and most trusted people in our childhood. We begin learning right from wrong and gradually start mimicking our parents. Soon after, our social circle increases, and we begin making friends. We start learning from them by what they say and how they act. And then we start becoming influenced by society whether we recognize it or not. Especially with the immense power of social media, it is inevitable to avoid it. At a much larger scale, we start seeing what's popular and what's accepted or normalized.

We already know how significantly our parents impact us. As for our friends, we typically are or become those who we associate ourselves with. That being said, choose wisely! Your friends do reflect you to a certain extent, so make sure they align with your level. Our friends will influence is in either a positive or a negative way. They will either lift us up, plateau us, or bring us down, whether it be conscious or subconscious to us. Since we become more independent in high school through college, this is around the time we start making our friends more like our second family.

I personally believe that the people you hang out with reflect your self-worth to a degree. I had to distance myself from a lot of people for the sake of my well-being and knowing that I was settling from who I was hanging out with. In my case, I now have higher standards because of the extreme value I price my time at. This is why successful people surround themselves with other like-minded successful individuals. If you want to hang out with people for the sake of hanging out with them, go ahead. Who am I to judge? Some people want to grow and self-improve while others want to stay at the same level they are always at. It's really up to you to decide how you want to go about your life.

Let's talk about loneliness as this is a very important talk that so many people including me face. I experienced *many* times of feeling lonely because of the lack of friends I had. On my solo trip to New York in December of 2019, I told myself that I needed to stop saying that I was fine living my life like a hermit. I was making excuses to myself. I realized that sometimes my extrovert to introvert ratio was out of balance, and that I truly am a very social person. Don't get me wrong, I really do thrive when I am alone which happens almost every single day. There is just a balance that I needed to maintain to feel my optimum self.

Experiencing loneliness is an inevitable part of the journey to success. Every day, you have to set aside focus and alone time for the sake of working on your future and self. And many times, your parents, friends, and others around you simply won't get it. That is okay.

We must differentiate between feeling lonely and being alone because these are two different concepts. Learning to be alone without any distractions and thriving while you're at it is an extremely game-changing skill to master. This is where we can be most focused and lock down on what we need to accomplish. Phone on airplane mode, we don't need to check it every hour, and it feels so relieving when we don't. Not only should we work on being alone with a task at hand, but also simply by ourselves when we are reading, praying, and doing anything that helps to nourish and replenish our spiritual needs. This needs to be a priority no matter how "busy" our lives may get.

Don't worry about making friends or finding people, the right ones will come into your life, you just need to be patient. The same goes with whoever you are destined to marry! He or she will come into your life at the right moment and time. This is something that cannot be forced or sought after. Trust in God and pray to Him whatever your heart desires.

Another thing to be aware of is peer pressure. I see it be more common with boys as they tend to do the craziest things to try to impress their friends. It's like all respect goes right out of the window. Falling into peer pressure has a lot to do with insecurity, which is why there is a need in the first place to want to impress someone. If one was actually secure, they wouldn't feel compelled to act out and try to get recognition from others. So, there is that direct peer pressure, but like I mentioned before, there is also that giving off of energy also at play. If we aren't aware, we won't even notice that we are slowly starting to become who we surround ourselves with whether it be a good or bad thing. If you have a group of friends who gossip like it's their job, you will most likely start imitating them even if you don't notice it at first. The more you hang out with people who behave and act differently than you do, the more you start catching up to their lingo, ambience, and behavior. You start becoming like those who you surround yourself with. Therefore, just be aware when you do so. Are these the type of people you want to surround yourself with? Are they elevating you or bringing your spirits down?

No matter what, stay true to yourself and know that compromising your morals to please someone else will not end too well. You don't have to do this, at all. By "stay true to yourself," I mean to remove the ego and to align yourself with your personal beliefs instead of conforming to what other people think you should do or what others tell you to do. If you ever feel like you are getting negatively influenced (and this is something your intuition can tell you based on the way you feel when you are around these people), do not be afraid to cut them out of your life. It comes down to who you value more, yourself or the people around you? In order to grow, all of the garbage must be taken out!

That's it for friends, now let's talk about society. I see society as a "collective judgement of the masses," and each individual, of course, plays a small role in it. The unfortunate thing is that the values and norms of society tend to be quite misleading and may throw many people off guard. For example, when a new trend appears, it becomes a domino effect of everybody trying to also be a part of it without considering if they are being true to themselves. If society tell us that a certain body type is "in," then what happens to the other people who don't have that specific body type? What are we *really* trying to say? We even had something on social media called "cancel culture," which is when an individual, usually a celebrity or public figure, openly gave their opinion on something or did something "wrong" and "offensive." As a result, a thousand internet trolls who strongly disagree with that opinion or behavior would begin condemning them by commenting something like, "cancelled." This is a great example of a bad trend and one that is extremely unhealthy. Side note…isn't it so ironic that when someone who is well-known makes a mistake, they get brutally and publicly criticized over that one or two things of "wrong" they did, meanwhile the people who "cancel" them act like they have never made a mistake in their lives? The lack of empathy is real. *All* of us have made a big mistake at some point or at many points of our lives, and I am undoubtedly positive that none of us would want to get publicly condemned and borderline harassed.

That being said, please be aware of society's negative tendencies that are very indistinct and make sure to never conform with something you don't agree with. To follow the path of the masses may be a dangerous road to be on, which is why it is so important to have awareness. In a place that can turn so good to so dark in a blink of an eye, we should always spread love and support each other whenever we can.

Chapter 8

The Unfulfilling Chase

"Man is not what he thinks he is, he is what he hides."
--André Malraux

Going off of my last chapter, I felt inspired to speak on something that I have so much passion for spreading awareness about. The unfulfilling chase.

Very fortunately, I have experienced and learned from this at a young age. I know that some people aren't as lucky to have received wise pieces of advice from some of the greatest people on Earth like I have, so it is my great duty to share it with you right now. I know that everyone grows up with different perception, but I think that collectively as a society, we value certain things that shouldn't be put on a pedestal.

Especially in the age of social media, it seems to be more prevalent than ever. If it truly is or isn't, I am not sure, but what I do know is that it is much more easily exposable because we have the world at our fingertips. Something that I have enjoyed hearing about from my favorite person ever, Gary Vaynerchuk, is about our insecurity and the way most of us mask it.

We compare way too much, and it results in pure unhappiness and dissatisfaction with ourselves.

We can see somebody with a more athletic looking body than we do, compare, and not *feel* good enough.

We can see somebody much wealthier than us and begin to feel scarce and like we don't *have* enough.

We could be grinding away with our work and see someone that seems to have gotten overnight success and feel *discouraged* without knowing that they probably spent many years to get to where they are at.

We could see someone with fame and feel *inferior* because we assume that having "more" results in being happier, more fulfilled and complete without knowing that most of these people are actually miserable on the inside.

Well, I am here to tell you that all of these things aren't what many of us think they are and what they really do. Any chase of anything outwardly will create a false notion of security and completeness. For most people, wanting and acquiring "more" actually starts a very toxic process because of attaching their self-worth by their accomplishments, financial gain, and followers. I am not saying these things are inherently bad because they are not. Many people just make them out to be from having a misconstrued intention.

"I would be happier if I had more money."

"I would be more lovable if I had a nicer body."

"I would set myself up for fame if I just get this one opportunity."

"I would be much more confident if I looked like her."

"I would be much less lonely if I had a boyfriend/girlfriend."

No, no and no. It isn't about who looks like what or who has more than you. More of anything will *not* make any positive difference, it will most likely just more of how you are currently. Have you ever heard someone say that being drunk doesn't change your morals, it just enhances more of who you already are? When I first heard this, it genuinely shocked me, but it really did make sense. Therefore, your sadness won't go away if you had more money, it would actually just make you more sad. No body shape will solve your deeply rooted insecurities. And yes, getting yourself into a relationship to fix your personal issues won't end well either. I will give it to you though, it will help temporarily. This is why we all call it "temporary happiness," it lasts for a very limited amount of time until you are right back to where you were. This isn't anything to aim for because we should want to do and be better than that. Self-love, hello?! We should want to chase something that is so beautifully fulfilling rather than an easy to fix solution that only covers the problem.

We go on social media and see seemingly perfect people with the perfect skin, nails that match their outfits, and all of these outrageous curves. The toxic comparison process starts. The more you scroll, the more people start looking the same to you with their "perfection." Some of the most popular comments I see on social media are girls saying, "if I had a body like that, I wouldn't know how to act." Sister, you are perfect with the body you already have. It isn't about your measurements or proportions, it's about acceptance and making a vow to yourself that you will love your body no matter what shape it is in. And let me get this straight, you can love and value your body and still have the desire to improve it through working out. You can do whatever your heart desires, but just make sure your intentions align with your truest and most authentic self.

To avoid comparing yourself to others, I highly recommend to just "stay in your own lane" meaning mind your own business! We don't need to know nor care what goes on in other people's lives. Truth be told, most people put on a show anyway, which gives us another great reason to simply not care. It's also best not to judge, because we really just don't know what is going on behind the photo or closed doors. Either way, we should know that more often than not, it's a deception many people create to show everyone else how "cool" or "perfect" looking their lives are.

I used to catch myself become so disheartened looking at all of these people with so much money, luxury, friends, and what seemed to be an overall flawless life. It wasn't a rare occurrence when I would stalk some member from the Kardashian-Jenner family and just feel sad because of "how far away" I was from them.

Long story short, I cut those negative thoughts from my life and began fully becoming aware of the fact that I was on my own path to success, and it didn't matter how anybody else's looked like. It's important to realize that there will always be someone who has "more" than you, but as long as you know your purpose and work hard towards it, all of those distractions shouldn't matter. Another tip is to stop following or "stalking" anyone who doesn't inspire or motivate you. It's quite simple!

What happens so often is that when we chase something, whether it be fame, money, drugs, alcohol, sex, attention, power…we fall short and will continue doing so *every single time*. Sure, it may be temporarily satisfying, but it will never bring peace. I've said this more than enough times, right? Well listen to something that I find to be very enlightening.

Some people call it "spirit," you can use whatever word you want to call this intangible "Thing" that is inside of us because it's all the same. God made us in His image out of love, and therefore we have love within ourselves too. We were made in love. Our entire spirit is love.

Anything that doesn't resonate with that will of course bring never bring fulfillment; the chase of fame for reputation, money for status, usage of drugs and alcohol to make you temporarily forget about reality, the desire for sex and/or sexual partners to feel complete, whole, and free of any void or loneliness. There's also the internal longing for someone to make us feel loved and needed, as well as the desire for power to attain false superiority over others. Just to name a few. All of this really is the masking of deeper issues like being insecure, feeling lonely, lacking self-love and love for others. Nothing less. All of our desires point to something greater, something Divine. Something that only God can wholly satisfy.

For being 19 years old, I made quite a bit of money and was unsurprisingly the least bit fulfilled. In the beginning of 2019, I made a personal goal to hit a certain amount of money in revenue by the end of the year. Soon after I set it, I saw a new video posted by Gary Vaynerchuk. I don't quite remember everything he said, but he essentially talked about why we play this miserable game of chasing things just to try to appear "cool." I naturally love listening to advice, inspiration, and all of that type of stuff as long as it's truthful, and this video in particular hit home. I began working on my ego and started asking myself what my intention was about setting this money goal and if my heart was *truly* in it.

My heart wasn't into it at all, and I had no genuine desire for it because my intentions were wrong. I realized that chasing something without a reason benefiting a greater good would get me absolutely nowhere and was the perfect recipe for an unhappy life. That day was when my perception of money totally changed along with the materialistic things that money can buy. I began working on myself and slowly letting this mixed belief go that I had to buy and wear certain things or look a certain way to feel accepted. Now, I have close to no care in the world.

Trying to fit in, going to parties, talking to the wrong boys, and caring about my status led me away from my childlike self that was innocent, good and loving. The desire for fast fame made me post pictures that did not reflect my personality and show who I truly was at my core. I didn't mean to, but I put myself in a box and got labeled for it. When I tried getting out of the box, there were people who didn't like it and called me names, doubted me, and said some really mean things. It still happens too.

I held onto the desire of wealth so I could feel validated and important, but that got me nowhere. The more the ego, the less of love there is. Settling with boys who treated me poorly because I had no love for myself. The partying, drinking, and the recklessness only masked the lack of value I had for myself. There is always something deeper going on. And yeah, I am open and raw talking about my past and how I used to be. My past will *never* define me because I know who I am now and the change it took to make me get here. Ain't nobody telling me otherwise!

So that's that...the unfulfilling chase. At the end of the day, we have a choice. Whether you want to wake up and repeat the cycle of lusting over meaningless things or start fresh and begin working on a better and happier self is all up to you. And like always, there will be times when you stumble and fall, but as long as you get back up, forgive yourself and continue on, you will be unstoppable.

Chapter 9

2 Different Types of Fun

"Let the rest do whatever, while you do whatever it takes."
--Grant Cardone

This topic will be of significant value, especially for the young adults. I believe that there are two types of fun, and while it is more of a subjective topic because everyone defines "fun" in their own way, I think it will be great to look at the two sides of it. Both of them are very different and have different after-effects. Also, this isn't me shaming or praising one form over the other. At the end of the day, what matters is what makes *you* truly and genuinely happy and fulfilled.

One will inevitably draw you further to a more fulfilling life and one will leave you questioning if there even is more to life. One will leave you thanking God and the other will leave you feeling emptier than before. One is encouraged by society and the other gets questioned. "Do you even have fun in life?"

I have gotten many questions asking me if I miss partying and if I feel like I am "missing out" from the college lifestyle that almost every student goes through. The staying up late, partying it up with friends, drinking alcohol, and everything else that falls into being a young adult. This would be one example of the short-term fun I will talk about.

The short answer is no, and I will explain why. Personally, I never really once gained satisfaction coming home from a party. Not that kind of soul-satisfying feeling that comes from experiencing joy, communion with others, beauty, and peace. Experiencing both forms of fun, I can say that one made me feel significantly better than the other. Sure, going to a party always got me "hyped up," but I think my ego was doing most of the talking. I always left feeling like I could've spent my time on something better for myself. That's just how I am. I felt like I was missing something and that there was this unavoidable void. I always had that voice telling me that this isn't where I should be.

Not too long ago, I was in Australia to tour Sydney and to attend a fitness expo in Melbourne later. The team and I had a nice dinner with drinks, and we altogether decided to further pursue the night by going to a bar. Keep in mind, the drinking age there is 18, so I was good! There was that part of me that got "hyped up," but it very shortly ended as we actually got there.

Something switched off in me, and all of a sudden, I wasn't feeling all that great despite trying to live in the moment and enjoy a night out. I was unhappy. That voice crept in again saying that I shouldn't be here and that this was a waste of time. About 15 minutes in, I decided to stop trying to force it, so I went back to my hotel room.

Now, I don't want to assume that everyone feels this way, but I think most of us have at some point in our lives. There were probably several variables that served as a catalyst for me to leave, but I noticed that when I get honest with myself, this is how I feel, especially when there is little to no benefit of me attending. Since I have reached that point of significantly valuing my time that if something doesn't give me a positive ROI (return on investment) then I simply don't want it. It becomes rather meaningless for me.

However, please do not misunderstand me and think I am saying that going out is bad. I am simply speaking from my perspective. I think it all depends on who you are as a person and what your goals are. Your goals need to match your actions. If you want to become highly successful yet you fool around and go out every single weekend, then you know deep down that there are many other people outworking you. There are people out there who are hungrier than you are, and it will show. That's the hard truth. It is your choice of what you want to sacrifice in your life to get you to where you want to be.

I call the type of fun that most people often participate in, "temporary fun." Whether it be spending way too much time with your friends, doing drugs, fooling around with multiple people, playing games all day, disrespecting your body, partying often and having or doing too much of anything. It's unfortunate, but it is somewhat an expected behavior for a young adult to do. What I just listed would be considered a standard. Some people have the mindset that they will have this fun all four years of their college experience, and then "figure it all out" after they graduate. By now, we should all know that this is a lie we tell ourselves to avoid breaking out of bad habits and working on ourselves meaningfully.

What I listed doesn't progress anyone where they say they want to go. You cannot have a desire for all of the things you see successful people have but not work on developing yourself first and foremost. It's delusion when people want all of these things and get angry or upset that they don't have it, but their execution shows otherwise. We must hold ourselves accountable. What do you really want? Are you willing to sacrifice things and people that hinder your potential?

On the other end, there is "fulfilling fun." It's the type of fun that will replenish and bring joy to the soul. It usually contains some form of investment towards the bettering of yourself or a selfless act made in love. Participating in it gives you a sense of peace and contentment. It's a healthy balance that makes life beautiful and enjoyable. It makes you love yourself and everyone around you better and elevates your spirit. You sense God's loving presence and you feel very deep satisfaction. How beautiful.

You do not have to be in company to have fun, you can have fun being by yourself, obviously. This is something I do on a daily basis because I prioritize myself. In other words, I value my time *a lot.*

For getting work done, I love going to either the library, a coffee shop or Barnes and Noble. Anywhere with not too much noise and distraction is wonderful for me. Every Sunday and sometimes during the week, I will go to Mass which replenishes me and gives me a spiritual high. There is something so special about communal worship, it can have such a tremendous impact. Most people are singing, worshipping, and feeling a great love within. The ambiance just makes you feel so good! My soul craves it more and more.

I also love and highly appreciate spending time with intellectual and like-minded people; I am so blessed to have some people around me who I can learn from and feel at peace with. I even pray for more of this, more like-minded people to surround myself with. It's extremely hard finding young women around my age who share the same goals, dreams and drive as I do. Very, very hard, but I know that God will send me the right people in due time.

My fun time is often found in my alone time. You can experience joy anywhere you go, it just takes gratitude, being present, and embracing everything with love, which is a big portion of what spirituality is.

The main difference between these two types of "fun's" is how it makes you feel afterward. The ultimate question you should ask yourself is "Does it give you regret, or does it make you grateful?" Be honest with yourself. Could you be spending your time in better ways? If so, start cutting out all of the things that do not make you feel complete or content.

Too many people are stuck in the same routine. Let's take weekends for an example. Many people wake up with their mornings almost over, waste time on their phone, maybe do something productive for an hour or two, go hangout with their friends in the evening, stay up on their phones scrolling through social media past midnight, and then go to sleep. Sometimes this might happen every single weekend and maybe even on a weekday too. We shouldn't be slaves to our phones or anything that robs us off of our meaning and purpose. So many people are living corpses trying to find life in "temporary fun" and then being irritated as to why nothing "good" is coming out of their lives. Remember, match your actions according to your goals, otherwise you will just be a dreamer that dreams without producing anything. Invest more of your time in fulfilling fun, nobody is going to do it for you.

Chapter 10

Coming Back to Where We Started

"We must go beyond the constant clamor of ego, beyond the tools of logic and reason, to the still, calm place within us: the realm of the soul."

-Deepak Chopra

When we stray away from our childlike selves, it is up to us to come back to it (only when we are willing to change and right our wrongs). By saying "childlike," I do not literally mean how children act, but I mean the pure, free, and fearless state of mind we originally once had. This includes freedom from fears and not having prejudice or bias — only love. Being ambitious, passionate and driven to do the things we wanted to do without much care about what might go wrong. When someone upset us, they would be easily forgiven. It's fascinating that children around the preschool age are very much unknowingly connected to their inner selves because they haven't been heavily "domesticated" or influenced yet. The world didn't yet tell them that they couldn't achieve what they wanted to do.

I strongly believe that one of our life purposes is to gain awareness of the patterns and habits we picked up from the world and begin the process of reverting back to how we began, to become childlike again. To find that passionate, loving, ambitious, driven, carefree, and optimistic state of being again. This is definitely harder for some people who had certain fixed beliefs engrained in their minds for a long time or traumas that seem difficult to overcome, but it is very much possible.

- The 3 steps to change are: having awareness, having the desire to change, and taking action. We cannot have one without the other, otherwise it won't work. Let's break these 3 down.

First, you have to become aware of who you are at the present moment, be honest with yourself, and acknowledge anything that you might not like about yourself at this point in your life. Really take some time to reflect, especially on your weaknesses and your wrongs. Bring back what is making you suffer and all of your untouched traumas and mental wounds. Many people do not like going into the ugly parts of themselves, they would rather put that off for "later" or completely disregard it. Change will never happen if you are not honest with yourself. As many of us wish we could, we cannot trick our hearts. It's for our own good to expose the ugly, expose the pain, and expose our failures, so then we can get to healing the right way.

Second, you must have the desire to change. You have to be 100% serious and determined, otherwise you will eventually fall back into the same routine. Without this force of desire, you will never change. Do you really want it? If so, how bad do you want it? How badly do you want to succeed? To win? To attain happiness? If you don't want it, you will never get it. Being determined will result in great things because the more you want it, the more you will believe in it, which means the more likely you will manifest it in your life. Also, I thought it would be important for me to add that we cannot change other people. They *have* to desire this. It is found from within. You can do everything and anything for that person, but if they lack that inner desire and drive, nothing is going to happen.

Third, you must take action and start instilling discipline. A feeling is not enough to elevate you to the place you want to be, this is why relying on motivation will fail in the long-term. Discipline gets formed through consistent repetition. The thoughts in your head that say, "maybe next time," "you can start tomorrow," "this isn't that important," and "you won't be good enough" need to be ignored. Forming discipline requires overcoming mental battles, even on a daily basis. Also, a plan for execution is essential because nobody can aimlessly go about doing something without having somewhat of a game plan. What are you going to do and how are you going to do it? <u>Your plans might change throughout the months or years of execution but always make sure that the *why* or the intention stays the same.</u>

Write down what you want, how you think you will get there, and execute through your daily actions. Not every step you take may be in the right direction, and that is good because that is where you will learn and will hopefully learn about patience too. Every step you take is bringing you closer to your final destination, but just make sure to enjoy the journey while you're at it. Anything really good in life will take years and years to attain and make sustainable.

It really is a shame when people want to do or start something, and then never do it. This is due to so many reasons, but let's describe this feeling deriving from something so deeply rooted within us, fear. Taking action is probably the hardest part of the 3 steps because it isn't easy breaking out of a habit, comfort zone or a fixed way of thinking. We may even be afraid of what our friends, family, or society will think of us. Or what if we start something and fail? Or what if we are so afraid of the unknown? These are all comments stemming from fear that need to be overcome unless you would rather stay the same.

We like to overthink, but being realistic...what is the worst thing that can happen? We fail, learn from it, become more knowledgeable, pat ourselves on the back for trying, and maybe attempt something again. Or maybe some person criticizes us but then again that says much more about them than you. The more you do things that make you feel uncomfortable, the more you grow and gradually begin defeating that fear within you.

Take someone that inspires you or who you personally admire and follow their footsteps to an extent. See what they do, how they think and talk. One powerful piece of advice that I learned was that you don't need to have an actual mentor who is present, who calls you or most definitely who you have to pay (which I ended up spending a lot of money on for a very small ROI). Anyone that you look up to can become your mentor, you just have to do enough research about them and do some stalking on social media. More than ever, people are documenting their journey and speaking about their experience on all sorts of social media platforms. For example, I would most definitely consider someone like Gary Vaynerchuk to be my mentor even though he doesn't know that I exist (yet). Knowledge is abundant and there are thousands of success stories to look up to. Just use Google or go on social media, everything you need is already there.

We will never grow and become better if we stay in our shells. Don't you want the best for yourself? Don't you want to do something meaningful? Don't you want to look back and not feel a deep feeling of regret?

We all know those people in our lives that constantly talk about doing whatever they want to do, and they never really do anything. This might even be ourselves. Try to distance yourself away from people like this if your goal is to grow. We should be more "doers" than we are talkers.

It is time for you to step up, come face to face with fear and defeat it. Anybody in the world can do this primarily because our fears are created in our minds, it is all a mind game. There is no luck, there is no "they were born this way," and there is no shortcut. Nobody successful has ever said, "Ah, I am going to sit back and rely on luck to help me out of my situation." It would've been much easier for everyone if life worked that way, but it fortunately doesn't.

Motivation is BS. One of the most popular questions I receive is how I stay motivated. I don't. It's when the internal discipline takes over and does the things you know you have to do even when you don't want to do them. It is going to the gym even when you are tired. It's waking up early in the morning even when you want to get an extra hour of sleep. It's working towards your goals even if you don't feel like working. It's not going for that unhealthy food even when the temptation seems inevitable. It's not texting that certain person knowing that he/she will disrupt your peace or cutting someone out of your life for your sake. It's about saying no to the things that you know will hold you back from achieving your fullest potential. And if you fail, which is inevitable, you must get back up again. Quitting is not an option, don't even think about it.

Chapter 11

Forgiveness

"Forgiveness is giving up the hope that the past could be any different."
--Dr. Gerald G. Jampolsky

Forgiveness is an extremely beneficial act that I heavily implement in my life. It takes complete mental and emotional effort since it begins with accepting what happened, letting it go, and finding peace with ourselves and the situation. It isn't easy, but it is by far very rewarding and life changing. Sooner better than later, we need to let go. The act of forgiving is the highest form of self-love that we can give ourselves, because we can't fully love ourselves if we are still holding onto pain, anger and resentment.

Let's face it, we have all been let down, betrayed, and disappointed. Some betrayals are worse than others, of course, and the worst ones hit us the hardest and stay with us the longest. Literally speaking, deep wounds take a long time to heal. We use creams, antibiotics and bandages to treat these wounds, and then we are left with a scar. It's the same with emotional wounds, it takes time and a consistent application of forgiving, meditating or praying, and working on ourselves until the pain becomes a memory without emotional baggage. That's when you know you have completely forgiven someone, when there aren't any negative feelings left.

Obviously, not all of us want to forgive those who have done us wrong. It's harder than holding a grudge because of the many emotions that come into play, the awareness that it will take more time to work on, and some people would rather hold onto pain than go through the process of letting go. Most people cover up their suffering with all sorts of fluff, like having sex with many people, popping pills and getting wasted, working nonstop, binging on food, projecting their negative emotions out on other people, etc. These actions are all temporary solutions, which only prolongs the problem.

Forgiveness takes courage and mental fortitude, but on the bright side, all of us can access it, and you can start today. Unfortunately, many people associate forgiveness as being weak and having a negative connotation on it being a feminine quality. Actually, the emotional body is a type of feminine energy but that does *not* mean we are talking about gender. All of us have a mix of feminine and masculine energies. For example, I have both of these energies because I am very assertive, goal-oriented, driven, dominant, but I also do possess qualities such as empathy, kindness, open-heartedness, intuition, and authenticity. This is having the mix of masculine and feminine energy. So back to what I was saying, forgiveness is *not* a weakness, it's very much a strength.

How we choose to feel now is a choice. The past cannot be altered, but the present can be changed, and the present is all we really have. Yes, people can do awful things. Yes, people can lie, lie and lie some more. Yes, some people can be cold-hearted. Yes, we probably don't deserve most of the hurt we carry. But everything that happened has already happened; it's done. It happened to teach us an important life lesson and make us stronger and wiser. If we hold onto that negative energy within, it will manifest right back into ourselves in endless cycles. Doesn't that sound like a big waste of time where growth could've taken place instead?

Life becomes a whole lot better when we release the pain, bitterness, and sadness. Realization is a necessity for change. It is not an overnight process, just like anything else worthwhile in life. Prioritize loving yourself and release anything that is getting in your way. By doing this, your entire world and perception of the world will change.

As I talked about in the chapter about senior year, I was in a very toxic relationship that wore me down mentally and emotionally. Most of the time I was unsatisfied, sad, and anxious. None of my emotional needs were met, and there were probably more arguments than actual conversations. All I wanted was to be treated the way I deserved to be treated.

Finding out that I got cheated on was just the cherry on top. A rotten cherry. I wanted to get revenge because I was so angry and full of anxiety that I nowhere near deserved. Keep in mind that I had a low level of self-awareness at this time in my life, so it was truly the best I could do and feel at the time. Many thoughts were running through my mind.

"How could he possibly do this to me?"

"He told me that he would never cheat on me."

"I want to expose him for the person he really is."

"I want him to feel what I feel."

I most definitely had a wrong approach to it, and there was nothing loving or compassionate about it. Like I said, it was the best I could do. Peace be with him.

I like to think of my story of forgiveness as beautiful and the most pivotal moment of my life. Without getting into too much detail, a girl that knew me sent a screenshot that related to my ex-boyfriend, and all of my hatred inflamed because of the utter lie I just saw. I became so disgusted that I messaged him about what a horrible person I thought he was. Not long after that, the anxiety started, so I stopped pouring my poison and blocked him again. I felt awful and a part of me couldn't believe how out of control I felt.

The morning after was life changing. I realized that I had so much pain and resentment inside of me, that I wanted it all gone. I was over the battle I was holding on internally. So, I did what I wanted to do for a long time…I reached out to God, genuinely this time. I even began playing my Worship playlist on Spotify and began crying it all out. I asked God to take away the pain and negativity, to help me forgive my ex-boyfriend and to heal me of my unresolved pain. I was so broken and emotionally lost. I was hurt and betrayed and needed love from the source of love Himself. Human affection and care are powerful and essential, but nothing can compare to God's care and love. I was letting it all go, and I knew God was right there with me. This probably took around 45 minutes.

Truth is, yeah, I was hurt.

Yeah, I was immensely betrayed.

I was struggling.

I was crying.

I was anxious.

But that was all okay. I was willing to experience all of these feelings and go through them over and over again (which I did) to get me to a place of healing and forgiveness. I chose self-love. I chose the long and hard route, and from that I found God, purpose, happiness, peace, and overall became the young woman I am today. So yes, it is very much worth it.

There is a greater purpose to everything, especially in our suffering. Like I said before, we naturally have a very limited perception and understanding of when negative things happen to us. Our initial reaction may be something such as, "Why is this happening to me? I don't deserve it." Deserving something or not, that shouldn't matter. God puts obstacles in our lives to be overcome and to teach us valuable lessons. He doesn't put them there to punish us or scold us, it is most likely due to our own stubbornness. When we don't follow our intuition, we will get many signs that we shouldn't be heading in the direction we are whether they are internal and external. Kind of like how most of us ladies, if not all, have experienced all the red flags in the world about some guy yet still choose to ignore those flags. We keep pursuing it until we get hurt. Remember that? That's what I'm talking about.

I kept sticking around in a relationship I had no business being in because of how I was being treated, and I most definitely learned the hard way out of that one. But sometimes, it doesn't to happen like that. You may experience a wakeup call in multiple other ways. Sometimes, you just have to accept with what you're given or suffering with and transform it into something beautiful and meaningful. It's better to do that than complain about it, right?

We grow stronger and love harder when we surmount difficulties either with ourselves or with other.

Everything happens for a reason. God is omniscient (all-knowing), so what He may know, we might not even understand of in the present moment. But that day will come when you will reflect, put the puzzle pieces together, and find peace in knowing that what happened was essential to be where you are now.

When you begin to let go and forgive, it doesn't even come close to an overnight process. With that comes failing, getting down, and getting back up again. It took me over a year. The beginning is hard with very frequent ups and downs, and then it slowly starts getting better, then worse, and then better again. That's how it goes, you can be doing well for some time, and then bam! Something happens and you feel like you are backtracking or staying stagnant in your progress. With every setback I've had, I have gotten back up from it and felt even better than I had before.

I follow a wonderful young Christian woman named Sadie Robertson who stated someone so perfectly, that it would be a shame if I didn't mention it in this book. Sadie said, "What time does is that it fogs things for a little bit, makes you forget about it from time to time, but whenever somebody's name comes up, whenever something's right in front of you…if you feel a drop in your stomach, if you don't feel peace, if you feel fear, then time did *not* heal. Unfortunately, relying on time won't fully heal you. Like I said, it's also praying, meditating, and forgiving which all ultimately results in taking *time* because it isn't a one-time action or reflection. We definitely learned another lie that time heals everything. That statement is not fully false, but it is missing a lot of fundamentals.

According to Newton's Third Law of Motion, for every action there is an equal and opposite reaction. Napoleon Hill talked about it, Oprah talked about it, and many others as well. This truth doesn't just apply to physics, it applies itself all throughout life. What's interesting is that it's universally known but phrased differently. Some call it by Newton's law, some call it cause and effect (karma), some say, "what goes around comes around," and others may say "you reap what you sow," but it all leads us to the same thing. I love how on point Oprah was when she said, "The energy you're putting out right now is coming back to you all the time whether you recognize it or not. And, if you can become conscious of that then it will change the way you operate your entire life." Amen to that, sister. For me, finding out about the cheating created an emotional downfall which was an "action" and later on my exponential growth was my "equal or opposite reaction." I had to hit rock bottom to shoot for the stars.

An important fact to note is that what anyone says or does to you is *not* because of you, but all due to what that particular person is going through or what baggage they hold in their lives. In Don Miguel Ruiz's book, *The 4 Agreements,* his second agreement is "do not take anything personally." This is one of the best and most powerful things that we can do for ourselves. Why? One reason is simply that the majority of human beings carry their own flaws, miseries and personal affairs onto other people through their words and actions. Many of these unresolved issues will manifest in ugly ways whether it be verbally, physically, or emotionally. Sometimes it could also be from a certain principle or way of thinking that they have engrained in their minds. If some people knew any better, they wouldn't behave the way they did. They were trying to do the best of their capabilities at that point in time, it's okay. That is why we shouldn't take anything personally.

Think about the people who take time out of their day to write hate comments or negatively criticize on someone they either barely know or don't know at all. I mean, who watches, reads or sees something and decides to comment with something rude? Most definitely not a happy person. The more these people hate and attack, the further they drift from their core state of being, which is made out of love. A happy person won't even consider spending the time being hateful, think about that. The best thing to do is show compassion and feel empathy for these people. Don't counter hate with more hate, that isn't the way to win. Forgive, love, and move on!

I actually came across a powerful truth in Robin Sharma's book, *The 5 AM Club: Own Your Morning. Elevate Your Life*. In his story, he said, "every human being does the best they can do based on the level of consciousness they are currently at and on the grade of true power they can command." Awareness is the key which leads to empathy because you know that this person's behavior, words and actions are a direct reflection on what's going on inside of them. On another note, if someone you care about says something unintentionally offensive, then confront them about it. There are some people who don't know what they said or did was wrong until it gets pointed out, which I have experienced in my life. Some people's actions are not made with caution and second thought, so don't think anything of it. It's a reflection of them, not you.

Fully forgiving is life changing. Imagine that you go through life carrying all of the negative emotions and grudges towards other people every single day...not so much of an enjoyable life. Imagine you keep track of all the people who have done you wrong, betrayed you, talked behind your back, lied to you, stole from you, bullied you, etc. You will soon become so heavy from carrying that load! Wouldn't it be great to take the first step and say, "God, free me from all of this, I want to become a loving person again. Help me to forgive all of these people who have wronged me at one point or another." Bam! Greatness and a clear sense of mind will begin to unfold.

We all make mistakes, every single one of us. Once we let go of the idea of perfection, that will help liberate us. Knowing this doesn't mean you should justify either you or the other person's behavior, but it will help you not live such a controlling life. And remember, most of our mistakes indicate to a lack of something deeper. We don't make mistakes just to make them, there's a reason to everything.

Anyway, let go, liberate yourself and watch yourself become the happy person you've always wanted to be. Choose to love and to forgive.

Chapter 12

Importance of Perception and Gratitude

"Be thankful for what you have; you'll end up having more. If you concentrate on what you don't have, you will never, ever have enough."
--Oprah Winfrey

Too many of us go through the motions, not acknowledging how blessed we truly are and how grateful we really should be. I struggled with gratitude for the majority of my life until I changed my perception completely. The reason for this is because I was never satisfied with what I had; I always thought that if I had more money, more status, and an overall better life that I would *then* give thanks. Because of this, I was never at peace, and it made me unhappy. I began to realize how blessed I am and how I am the choice maker of happiness. Outward possessions and titles meant nothing if my internal self was struggling to be grateful. I came to many realizations that made me become more thankful, but one of the biggest ones was the fact that there's at least someone who has it significantly worse than I do. Knowing this gives me absolutely no room to complain! It would also be a shame to disregard all of the blessings God has gifted me with and having this mentality will ultimately also close me off from receiving more.

If you are reading this book, you are already more blessed compared to billions of people in this world. It's true. No matter how bad someone thinks they have it, someone else is having it worse. Always remember that.

We know that we have a problem when our biggest concerns are the scandals that are going on with celebrities, just to give an example. We get easily sucked in by paying attention to other people's problems instead of focusing on our own lives. We will use any form of distraction to avoid doing things that progress us towards our goals. We settle with ourselves so much, and I really do think that we know it in our hearts.

Stay in your lane!

Changing our perception will change everything in our personal world. If we look at life as a positive, optimistic, and joyful creation, then we will feel that way. But, if we think of life as being dreadful, depressing and unfair, then we will feel hopeless and sad as well. On top of that, most people walk around without even having a purpose in their lives. I know that life becomes extremely meaningless if we just float around without a purpose or a definite goal because I used to feel this way. Don't you want something more?

Another possible cause of feeling discontent could simply be from a lack of gratitude. Gratitude is a game-changer. We live in a world where so many people are chasing "more, more, more," whether it be a bigger paycheck, notoriety, men or women, or better looks. It's rare that we stop and appreciate what we currently have, who we currently are, our health, our bodies, our safety, etc. We may even get into comparing our lives with others and feel a deep dissatisfaction because we aren't there. Maybe use this to inspire you, but don't get bogged down about this. You are on your own path.

We have the ability to make our lives a living heaven or hell. Life is a game of choice. I can choose to be happy and take the next steps of achieving it, or I can be sad and complain that my life isn't how I want it now. Form the habit of living in a state of gratitude, and if something unfortunate happens, give thanks for that too. As I said before, everything truly does happen for a reason, no need to look at things with a negative perspective.

How many of us are grateful just to breathe? To have a roof over our heads? Have water and food? A safe place to live? An endless amount of opportunities to create our lives the way we want them to be? I know you probably want to keep reading this book, but I want to include a quick prayer that you can use just to halt, breathe, and pray:

> Thank you, God. I genuinely and whole-heartedly mean this thanks. Thank you for giving me all that I need. I will begin acknowledging the importance of this on a daily basis. Thank you for my precious body that I will love, cherish, and treat as a temple. I will accept and love every part of my body. I am so blessed to have a safe and comfortable place to sleep every night. I am so blessed to be able to smell, see, touch, hear, and taste because I know that there are so many people who are less fortunate than I am. Help me never to forget these things. Help me to acknowledge all of the blessings in my life. Open my eyes, so I can see all of Your goodness and glory that You bless me with every day. Make me more aware of the next time I start taking my life and Your creation for granted because I do not mean to do so. And again, thank You God.

This is just a guideline, of course. The key points of praying and/or meditating is intention. You have to have a sincere intention and open state of mind. Try it out, I really think it will help. I know that to some praying may seem foreign altogether, which is totally okay. It was foreign once to me too, just as it was once to all of the Popes and monks at some point in their lives.

I know that there are people who will be quick to say, "it's harder for me because I have gone through such tragic events." Okay, I totally understand that. However, I don't think having an attitude like that will really get anyone far. Especially since for every problem you have, there has been a person who has overcame it and became successful. Therefore, it really shouldn't be a valid excuse. Don't limit your capabilities!

Chapter 13

My Faith

"Do not lie to each other, since you have taken off your old self with its practices and have put on the new self, which is being renewed in knowledge in the image of its Creator...but Christ is all, and is in all."
--Colossians 3:9-11

Faith played a huge role in my life. The purpose of this chapter is not to convert you or persuade you; I will just be sharing my story and how it impacts my day to day life.

Growing up, I never really learned about religion or spirituality, because my family weren't practicing Russian Orthodox members, even though some were baptized. I guess that just happened for "traditional reasons." I was baptized as a baby but growing up I had no idea what religion was about. There was no sense of who God was either, all I could think about was why He would let evil things happen in the world if He created it. I was filled with doubt and questions that nobody would answer without a negative bias. My mom actually took me to church about two times, and I remember it being way too long, too stuffy and having way too many elderly people. Even though the church was small, I also remember it being fascinating, beautiful and possessing grandeur at the same time.

Like everyone in certain points of their lives, I questioned many things concerning God (theology), human existence and the creation of life. Who is God? Who created the Universe? Why does He not show Himself to me, or anyone? Nothing made sense, and like I said, I had no real answers or another point of view. It was a lot of, "God, if I do something for you, will you give me this and do this for me?" To my disappointment, he didn't pop into my head and start talking like I wanted him to. It obviously wasn't just me, but most people carry many misconceptions and biases of who God really is, and I don't blame them one single bit. How can you blame someone who has no prior religious education nor grew up with that influence in their lives? This is why I ask all of you to go about reading these topics with an open mind.

Since God did not perform a miracle and drop-down chocolate from the roof like I wanted him to, I put Him in the back of my mind. As I mentioned at the beginning of the book, my mom pulled me out of public school and enrolled me in a Catholic school for 8th grade. It was one of the best things that have happened to me and was a pivotal point in my life. I was surrounded by a great community, great classmates and great teachers. Everyone seemed to be either very religious or had a strong knowledge capacity on theology. To go from a secular environment to a completely religious one was a major change. Everyone there obviously knew a lot about their faith, and I felt like I was the odd one out.

Thankfully, most people were welcoming and understood my nonreligious upbringing. We did short prayers every morning before class started, Mass every Tuesday, obligated theology class, and essentially everything I was not accustomed to. I was still indifferent to Catholicism because I had no foundation to go off of. Due to my parents' influence, I judged some of my classmates and their parents as being either way too strict, sometimes irrational, and too adherent to rules. But don't get me wrong, some parents definitely overdo it, but at that time I was in no place to set my judgment on something I didn't experience nor had much of an understanding on. However, it felt new and good, I was attracted to the idea of having faith and didn't completely reject it.

When having the option of going to either a public high school or a private Catholic school, I decided to continue my Catholic education. Fortunately for me, we were required to take "Introduction to Catholicism," which was yet another pivotal moment for me. This was the type of class I needed to catch up on the primary and basic knowledge of Catholicism.

Some time, after a couple of months, I experienced a conversion. I do not remember exactly what happened, but I believe I tried to pray properly for the first time, and God reciprocated. He reciprocated so greatly that I began to love Him more and more. I felt His goodness and I felt a different part of me begin to emerge. I felt happier and calmer, it was a feeling I had never experienced before because it didn't come from a particular person, thing or event. It came from my soul. For the first time, I believed in Him and knew He truly existed. My love and passion for God grew and deepened, I even felt peace!

This comes to show how important it is to have a foundation for anything in life. If I didn't take this class that helped me learn about the "basics" of Catholicism, who knows how long I would have stayed agnostic (a person who claims neither faith nor disbelief in God) for. You can't just jump into Algebra without having a solid foundation of basic math!

I never felt more at peace in my life. The only problem was that I wasn't really a "practicing Catholic" because I rarely attended Mass, Reconciliation (Confession), or had any form of communal worship. This actually really limited the extent to where my faith could go and how long it lasted because I was still in the beginning stages where I needed to be uplifted by people or a community. I was around 14-15 years old at that time, so I couldn't drive myself anywhere, and I felt extremely reserved to tell my parents about my love for God, knowing the type of unsupportive and snarky replies I would get.

One day, I was coming home so elated and excited from the aftereffects of going on a Catholic youth retreat. My parents asked me why I seem so happy, and I told them it was because of God, and they replied with something along the lines of me getting brainwashed and this being just a phase that I "will get over just like everything else." I don't think those comments affected me much, but I did feel disappointment in my stomach. It was a feeling coming from, "Why are my parents trying to crush my happiness?" Either way, I felt like it was their loss, not mine.

You see, I used to think believing in God and praying were a form of brainwash only because my parents told me so. I thought this way until I actually got a brain of my own and started thinking for myself.

I am empathetic to the people who say ridiculous and hateful comments against God or spirituality as a whole because it doesn't hurt anybody except themselves. We have been conditioned to think that there is nothing greater and more powerful to life than ourselves. That we are just flesh and bone ad were only put on this Earth to die one day. Some people even convince themselves that they are too smart to believe in something they can't see.

If you are one of those people, then honestly ask yourself how that's going for you.

A couple of months after I found out about the cheating, I sat on my couch and had a huge emotional breakdown. I was tired. Tired of the hate, tired of the anxiety, tired of feeling all of the negative emotions I felt for my ex-boyfriend.

"God, I am done. I am so done, and I am ready to go back to You. Please help me."

God is greater than all of humankind and greater than the potential power in any individual. Don't get me wrong, we have a ton of capabilities, but to receive love from the One who is made of it…is significantly different. I've felt it in my own life, others have too.

I was ready. I knew this next chapter was going to change my life forever. My love for God began increasing quite rapidly, and I began to go to Church just to sit and pray. A designated place of worship has a much different ambience compared to praying in your room, for example. Being in a holy area uplifts you.

I went to Mass and was actually present for the first time in years. I began going every Sunday, then a couple of days a week, and then almost every day for Lent. The amount of joy I had was night and day compared to the life I was living just over a year ago.

There is a very famous passage from St. Augustine's Confessions that says, "You have made us for yourself, O

Lord, and **our heart is restless until it rests in you.**" My soul was at rest. I knew what that felt like, and I never again wanted to participate in something that would not match that energy. Is your soul at rest?

God was forever stretching out His arms to me, and I finally took them. For good. Back then, I didn't know that in order to truly follow God, we have to fully submit ourselves to Him, which meant letting our past selves go. This is exactly what I did on that morning, but I wasn't aware that this had to happen until I started hearing more about it through testimonies and talks. It's recognizing that ache and crave in our soul and allowing for God to come in us and remove all our internal weeds (suffering, doubt, insecurity, anger, etc.) that hold us back.

It all makes sense as to why I couldn't seem to connect myself with Him again, and it was because I wasn't willing to leave my toxic behavior behind. I would pray for 5 minutes, and then go back to the same cycle the next day. My heart wasn't in it. It was all a part of a greater reason though; I had to hit rock bottom in order for myself to get back up again stronger, wiser, and with more purpose. Amazing.

He knows all and wants the best for us. It is essentially the same saying as "everything happens for a reason." It really does. Yeah, sometimes things don't go as I want them to. God knows all of our desires, but maybe we are not ready to receive the things we want. Or maybe we are simply not ready for them. Or maybe something doesn't happen because it was safer for it not to happen. Or maybe this loss, heartbreak, and temporary failure is going to change into something good and powerful that will teach us a significant lesson and make us stronger like it did with me. Have you ever thought as to why you aren't attracting what you want? Maybe it's because you haven't fully worked on yourself enough to attract those things or people into your life yet. Maybe you just have to give it a couple of more tries until God gives you that breakthrough.

We are not in control, to a very large degree, when it comes to how our lives play out; we tend not to see the bigger picture because we are naturally very limited in that regard. Only through awareness and a change of perception can we fix this limitation.

Anyway, that was my little story about how I experienced my conversion. Enough about me.

Please understand that I am not trying to convert you. I am simply sharing my perception and beliefs in hopes that it might open someone's eyes. As you can tell from what I shared about my past, I used to live my life with closed eyes too. It personally didn't get me anywhere. This chapter is the key to peace and equilibrium, or the "secret sauce" to the recipe for long-lasting happiness. Having a fit body and an even better mindset is fantastic, but in order to truly be your best self, the emotional and spiritual bodies also need to be in constant work. Do not disregard the spiritual body!

I think the pattern of our human behavior is easily recognizable. It is from living in a shallow way without any sense of spirituality as well as having an untamed emotional body that we see many people broken, lost, hedonistic, addicted and depressed. It is such a one-dimensional way of living life because of this absence. We are created for much more meaning besides living and dying. This meaning has to be given first in order for it to exist. God gave it, and He is a Divine power so much greater than all of humanity.

Just like how we constantly create things and give it meaning, so did God when He originally created everything. It's the same pattern. And God created us in His image and likeness, and therefore He shares a bit of Himself in us. It's all connected. When we constantly do things that go against what God wants us to do, we cannot help but notice that we fall short and feel unfulfilled every single time. What more can I say? When the dots are connected, it becomes so clear that there is Divinity, a higher power at work.

You do not need to know all of the facts and all of the most compelling reasons as to why God exists. I most certainly don't know all of them, but I do have a life-long journey of learning. My eyes opened up when I gained a sense of self-awareness and knowledge, and I really hope that through my story you gained a different perspective as well. I do not think talking about God simply is "enough," I think it is also describing what I truly feel inside with all of this.

I believe that our gut feelings are clear indicators whether what we are doing is right or wrong. For example, getting anxiety from talking to certain people is a clear indicator that there is something wrong. Connecting to God and praying, we feel contentment, peace, fulfillment, joy, love and goodness, a clear indicator that this is where we are called to be.

Our hearts are restless until we find rest in You.

Chapter 14

On a Path to Success

"I think it is possible for ordinary people to choose to be extraordinary."
--Elon Musk

Many people settle by not unlocking their fullest potential which is why we tend to hear successful people call this majority, "mediocre." This is not to say that someone is better than the other, please don't misunderstand that. It's simply saying that many people gave up on their dreams and chose to live a life of simplicity and comfort. There is absolutely nothing wrong with this, it just isn't where I want to be.

I think that the main underlying values of success includes constantly overcoming obstacles, defeating fears, and doing what you love and can be the best at. It's that "simple." As a natural result of this, wealth accumulates. Society tends to view success on a one-sided way, primarily focusing on the rewards such as the money, fancy cars, mansions, accolades, and fame, but that isn't even of primary importance. What's greater than that is the impact on people you make and if you genuinely wouldn't want to do anything else in the world except what you currently do. Those two are important. Oprah may be a billionaire, but we tend to first look at the huge change she has made to this world. Mother Teresa wasn't rich in terms of money, but her soul was so rich that almost everyone knows of her by her work. One of Gary Vaynerchuk's biggest impacts was encouraging business leaders and lay people to put happiness on a pedestal instead of money and what it can buy. Success, however, isn't only limited to well-known people. You can be a successful mother or father if that is your calling. Change doesn't have to be recognized on a global scale.

My true path to success started when I set my ego aside and reflected on what I really feel deeply about and if I believe it to be of importance to share to the world. I asked myself, "what and who do I deeply resonate with?" It was easy for me to find an answer because I already started advocating it. That's actually why I even started writing this book. I acknowledged how absolutely blessed I was with all of the events in my life forming me into something I repeat quite often in this book, and that is my "best" self. Of course, I am not where I want to be at and being your "most successful self" is a life-long journey, but it is always worth documenting. I believe that any potential change I can make in the world, I should go for. Anyway, I resonate with young adults and more specifically, young women. This is where I feel called to be at the moment, and what I do "behind-the-scenes" away from social media will unravel itself later in 2020. Yes, that is that business project I was talking about earlier.

We are all called to make a difference in our own unique ways whether on large or small scale. This is where having purpose comes into play. Find your purpose and don't give up on it. The reason as to why most people fail is because they quit. Here are some reasons:

1. Standing out is hard. Whenever you begin to advocate about something you feel strongly with and it goes against society's standard way of thinking, you will get critiqued. Some people don't develop enough thick skin to withstand the negativity even if their mission is important to them. An example could be somebody who is pro-life and supports that wholeheartedly. They will inevitably receive negative replies back from people who are pro-choice. Opposition discourages many people.

2. Temporary failure. This is also very discouraging for most. They see it as a major loss when it actually is a gain because of the valuable experience. Don't expect to succeed your first time at trying something new. It took Thomas Edison 10,000 tries before perfecting the incandescent electric light bulb, and we have people out here quitting after one attempt!

3. Lack of patience: People don't have enough patience to keep trying, they want to move to the next "fast" thing. All good things take patience. Most businesses take years to become sustainably successful.

4. Self-Doubt: Some people have such high amounts of doubt within themselves that it stops them from even going after what they want. Their lack of confidence and fear of failing is so powerful that it overcomes the goals they've planned. I've also dealt with and still sometimes deal with the "I'm not good enough to achieve this" mentality, but I also strongly know that I can achieve anything I set my mind to. Why? People have already done it before me.

5. Judgement from others. This is also another inevitable outcome that you can't run away from. At some point, people will make fun of you, say you are full of it, call you stupid, criticize you, doubt you, etc. Funny thing is, those people are going to try and become your friends when you start showing signs of success. Remember, what other people say about you is a reflection of them, not you. Don't listen to anyone except yourself and people who are close to your heart, they should support you.

I have heard of different percentages that categorize people into being a part of the "mediocre majority." Napoleon Hill said it was 98% of people, Hal Elrod said 95% of people, and other well-known achievers have said 99% of people. I don't think we can get an exact estimate, but either way these percentages scream "most people." You can just take a look into your personal life and observe the behaviors of strangers, friends and family and come to the conclusion that most of them don't seem to be happy and try to become better individuals. It's obvious because our internal manifests into our external meaning someone who is fulfilled and content on the inside, will radiate with joy and happiness on the outside. On the other end, if someone is suffering on the inside and not taking proper care of that, it will show by them being easily triggered and irritable, yelling, insulting, starting drama, getting offended, and/or by being depressed.

Many people have a misconception about happiness. It isn't just found when things are going well, when we receive presents, when people around us are nice, or when we feel satisfied with ourselves in the moment. That's very, very temporary, and we all know that life doesn't go as planned most of the time. There are many surprises, not everyone is nice, our mind can start getting insecure over something, or we might get stuck in traffic for an extreme amount of time. When this happens, we are no longer "happy." If we look more into this, we are subconsciously finding happiness in external things and anything external is always changing. It isn't stable. You can make happiness into a feeling, but if you are looking for long-term satisfaction, it needs to become a state of mind. This is a choice we make. Living in gratitude, contentment, and love will bring about this state of mind. So, as we know, most people around us are always fluctuating in their feelings.

In terms of becoming better individuals, anyone is also capable of this. I strongly believe that a truly successful person never gives up and stops working on themselves. By this, I mean constantly learning and doing anything that will make them better than who they were the day before. It could be through reading books, surrounding yourself with smarter people, or cutting out certain things in your life that are holding you back. Maybe also going to sleep and waking up earlier, going to that class you always wanted to go, or doing something out of your comfort zone.

We can *all* improve; it just takes making a commitment with yourself. Being at a certain age or having a certain amount of success doesn't mean you have "hit your limit." Albert Einstein said, "Once you stop learning, you start dying." Maybe a little bit exaggerated, but he certainly gets the point across. I would say once you stop learning, you become stagnant. I believe a huge key to living a happy and fulfilling life is by always creating movement and never being stagnant. By "stagnant," I essentially mean being absolutely glued to anything that doesn't serve you a higher purpose and never trying anything that makes you uncomfortable. How many young adults spend hours upon hours scrolling through social media and procrastinating their lives away? Too many. I believe this also plays a role in our mental health. The more time we spend on superficial things, then the more we will be prone to anxiety, depression, and other disorders in the like.

Once you attain a certain level of self-mastery, you want to share that with the world so other people can help themselves. One of our jobs as God's stewards is to help our sisters and brothers in need, and we are all a family, or should be at least. We are all in this race together, and gender, sexuality, race, ethnicity, skin color, and age does *not* matter. It shouldn't be a fight to success between you and other people, it should be you fighting your weaker self on a daily basis.

I learned that the annual income of the bottom 1% of earners in the world is $430,000, not a couple of million dollars as most of us may think. This number isn't even half of 1 million dollars. How many of us have once said we want to become millionaires? Most of us. This proves that being financially successful isn't all that easy as our words make it out to be. We want it, we try to get it, and then we realize it was much harder than we thought. Waking up early to have a successful morning routine is hard, overcoming bad habits is hard, developing a successful business is hard, starting anything new is hard, doing things you don't feel like doing is hard, working hard is hard, and not falling into temptation is hard. Also, failing and not quitting is hard, having a clean and balanced diet is hard, distinguishing between something temporary and something that will reward you in the long run is hard, and sacrificing "play" time with friends for building yourself and your business is hard. The path to success is clearly *hard*, which is why so many people will never get there. The beginning is the most difficult, but once you start to build up momentum and practice, it gets a little better. Until you hit a roadblock and need to figure out a way to go around it and improve, and the cycle keeps repeating itself. As long as you keep progressing and the line on the line chart keeps going up, that's ultimately what matters. It's that constant drilling of discipline to get better, do better and achieve better. Most people do not want to do the things I listed, or they do, but do not have enough willpower to get to it. Some people genuinely don't care, and do not want to set the bar high, which is totally fine. To each their own!

However, I strongly believe that every single person has the instinct to want to do better. If we examine human behavior, we obviously can come to the conclusion that we feel much better about ourselves when we are productive as opposed to being lazy and procrastinating. We feel better when we exercise instead of not doing any physical activity. Yet again, we have another indicator that there's something in us that drives us to self-improve. People really do care whether they say they don't, they just come up with any excuse as to why they can't. Distractions come up and bam! They have put their innate desires on the back burner. Most people condition themselves to such a mediocre and mundane routine that they forget what it feels like to have dreams and ambitions. Don't let that be you, you deserve better.

Here's one example of the discipline I had to instill into myself through struggle and constant effort. I used to *hate* waking up early, I just couldn't do it. I always applauded others who would do it and would even be a tad bit jealous. "What do they have in them for them to wake up so early that I don't have?" It was something about waking up before the sun was up that I couldn't wrap my head around. "How do people do it? It's literally still pitch black dark outside!" On weekends or days I wouldn't have school, I sometimes finished making my breakfast an hour before the morning was even over. I even remember driving past a Church I always wanted to go to and reading the announcements that said "8:00 a.m. daily Mass." I was like "Really? That is way too early." I had no motivation to rise early, and nine times out of ten, I felt so unhappy that I was wasting my entire morning by sleeping. Oh, and I would always wake up and spend around 20-30 minutes on my phone scrolling through social media too.

A couple of months into 2019 is when I started trying to wake up earlier than around 9:00 a.m. I tried 8:00 a.m.

which was uncomfortable for me at first. What still made me slightly irritated was knowing that some people have already began their days while I was just getting up to start mine. When I started having a deep desire to deepen my faith, I knew that I had to start attending daily Mass, not just Sunday Mass. There was a Catholic Church very close to where I lived that began Mass at 7:30 a.m. I knew I had to make some sacrifices again. I changed my alarm clock to 6:57 a.m., and this made me feel good. Even though it was three minutes before 7:00 a.m., I felt proud of myself! It did take my body and mind some time to adjust, and it started getting difficult because I wasn't consistent about it.

Long story short, I began challenging myself even more by setting the alarm clock further back. I reached a pivotal moment for my morning routine when I read the book called *Rise and Grind* by Daniel Paisner and Daymond John and learned that every single successful person in there woke up before the sun went up. That book inspired me so much, I knew I had to sacrifice once again. I also read that some people worked out in the mornings, which again, I *never* thought I would do. I usually went to the gym later in the afternoon.

I went all the way down to 5 a.m. Keep in mind I also had to adjust the time of when I went to bed to ensure I got my 7 to 8 hours of sleep. What a miracle compared to a year ago. I woke up, journaled and prayed, got my coffee and avocado toast, and then headed to the gym by 7 a.m. I loved it; it was the definition of my successful morning routine that set the tone for the rest of my day. I had to sacrifice and push through to improve in the area I was slacking in.

When we talk about success, excuses do not matter. Nobody even cares about your excuses except for those who are as stuck in them the same as you are. Nobody will save us from feeling too tired, too busy, too old, too young, too afraid, too poor, not smart enough, not "ready" enough or that we lack the opportunities, weren't born into a wealthy family, waited too long, didn't get lucky enough, and the list goes on. At the end of the day, these are just stories that people keep telling themselves to put the work that needs to be done further off.

Motivational speaker and author, Les Brown, couldn't have said it any better. To be successful, you must be willing to do the things today others won't do in order to have the things tomorrow others won't have.to want to swim against the current, but most of us won't get there. The journey to success takes sacrifice, particularly sacrificing everything that the majority does. I will talk more about this in the next chapter. We also have to give up our old ways, just like what it takes to follow God. We need to throw our care about other people's judgment out of the window.

Do you think that I would still have my social media if I cared about what some people thought of me? Or when my dad said "no" when I told him I wanted to start a business? When my parents told me I would fail, continuously? When my classmates started judging and making fun of me for getting into working out? I always did what I wanted to do. And even if I did fail, so what? We need to become aware that failing is not a loss. You either win, or you learn. We must stop worrying about other people's opinions, it's a complete waste of time. Follow Gary Vaynerchuk on social media if you need to get more convinced.

One thing I want to caution you on is about the mentality some people fall into when they start chasing success, the baggage that tends to be picked up along the way. This is why it is important to set intentions and ask yourself why you want success in the first place. The want of fast fame can do some damaging things such as manipulating and putting on different masks to fit in or please others. Some people become so obsessed with the chase that they would do anything to get there as fast as possible, even if it means going against their morals and self-worth. And when they attain something they want, they soon lose that gratifying feeling and want more. Most of these people do a lot of fronting, but also know that behind the masquerade, they are very much unfulfilled. This is why it is extremely important that we live an authentic life and become aware once we start noticing we are slightly heading in the wrong direction.

A while ago, I had a chat with someone famous, and he asked me why I haven't moved to Los Angeles since I was in the "social media influencer" industry. I truthfully told him that I didn't have much of a desire to move there, and that I currently like where I live. The cons outweighed the pros, even if LA was known to be the hub of celebrities, influencers, and famous people. He basically replied telling me that if I wanted to gain notoriety quickly, I would have to hang out and network with people who would help get "big" faster. Sure, it interested my ego for a couple of seconds, but I quickly humbled myself knowing that this wasn't what I wanted to do. I told him that the people who "clout-chase" typically have to compromise their morals for fame, and he agreed with me and said that it had to be done to get to the top faster.

I get it, I really do. It just wasn't me. I reached a level of awareness where the idea of compromising my morals to reach a higher number of followers felt so extremely superficial. It's all ego. I have more faith in myself and my goals than to have myself "fake it 'till I make it." Like I said, it's about the long-term process. We have such limited vision because we want more and we want it now, rather than enjoying the journey which will be more rewarding in the end. Notoriety really isn't worth giving up peace and authenticity, really. It's so easy to get lost in the chase.

Now that I mentioned that, we can continue with the path to success Something I see often is that people don't really know what they want in the first place.

At the young age of 15, I developed an obsession for fitness and turned it into a lifestyle as well as built a business around it. My entire life documentation on social media shows a story of my growth. I went from being all about fitness, to fitness and business, and now my two favorite things are business and entrepreneurship. I had such a huge spark of motivation to start bettering myself physically, and I pursued that spark which ultimately led me to where I am now. Of course, I experienced a lot of negativity from my parents when they saw that I was getting really involved at the gym. Some negativity came from my peers at school, but that probably stemmed from envy. Regardless, I still did what I wanted to do, because I was so crazy in love with working out. It was an absolute obsession of mine, no matter what the odds were.

My advice to you is to find that spark of motivation and pursue it. If you try it out, get in tune with yourself, and truly do not find it fulfilling, then you can always quit it and find something else. There's a difference to quitting something you desire to do, and quitting based off of you not liking it. Not everything we do in life we will like doing, but if it's something that has to be done, then you should keep trying and trying. For example, I played competitive soccer from around 6 to 14 years old. I absolutely despised the last few years because I was forced to play a sport I no longer liked. On top of that, I had no friends on the team, some of the girls bullied me, and nobody would even try calling me by my first name. I got nicknamed "Stash" because some coach decided it was easier that way. Going to practice was a chore. My dad transferred me to another team that was in a lower league, and even though I was much more appreciated and praised, I still didn't feel fulfilled. I finally convinced my dad that I was done, even though he kept calling me a quitter. Of course, I was going to quit something I felt miserable and soulless doing. The day I officially quit was one of the happiest days of my life.

To possibly find your passion or something you really want to do, you must form a habit of doing it first; you cannot quit what you started a couple of weeks in. Give it a couple of months and see how you feel after that. This will also train your brain to become more disciplined. Discipline gets formed in the days when you get up and work when there is no motivation left in the tank. That is how it is and how it has always been. You cannot bend or go against it, but only go towards it (if you want to be successful).

If you quiet down, remove meaningless distractions, and develop a deep sense of awareness, then I am sure that your soul will point you in the direction that you should be going towards. I believe that the problem isn't in us not knowing what to do, but it is in not listening to ourselves. Having distractions and purposefully overloading yourself with work will not result in you finding yourself. Distractions could be found in spending way too much time on social media, with your friends, partying, using drugs, binging, procrastinating, engaging in toxic relationships or friendships, and trying to find love in all of the wrong places. How do you think you are going to find what you truly want to do if you are constantly doing the opposite? Finding yourself takes time, especially alone time and doing things that actually help you to grow.

Our time is so precious, but yet we stall so much and try to do everything to get us to the "next exciting thing." I remember asking a woman who worked at a dermatology clinic a simple "How are you?" and she replied with "just trying to get the day over with." She isn't the only one who feels that way. Money can always be made but time cannot. Wake up with purpose. Breath with purpose. Walk with purpose. Talk with purpose. Live with purpose.

If you feel deeply for environmental issues, social justice issues, feminism, health, veganism, or whatever it may be, then why don't you try to go further into topics like these? If you have always wanted to take a yoga class or a real estate class...what's stopping you? What makes your soul happy? What have you always wanted to do? Prioritize these things. I struggle with it sometimes too! It's hard to do the challenging tasks and to constantly go out of comfort zones, but this is your life we are talking about. Own it.

A common reason for failure is putting off the things that we need to accomplish. In order to excel and become a high-performance person, it must be done. If you want to be in the top 1%, you have to do the things the other 99% of people aren't willing to do. Whenever you feel bogged down and unmotivated, remember this.

I use my planner almost every single day and write out everything I should do and everything I should focus on. This helps me stay organized and not fall into just "going with the flow" or relying on my brain to remember everything I want to do because that's impossible for me. I have thousands of thoughts a day going through my head, and whenever I have a good one I always either write it down or video record it. Since my goals are high and take much work, I need to utilize all of the working hours of my day. I strongly dislike going to bed feeling like I could've done so much more, so I make it a priority to get the most important things done first. Be rest assured that I most certainly do not have everything figured out in life…at all. Every single day I try to get better and learn from my mistakes. I have days that aren't as good as the days before, but what really matters the most is if that line is still progressing upwards. I do get stuck a lot, especially since I have been focusing on creating a new business that's very foreign to me. Every day I am trying to "figure things out," but if I compare that to even where I was last year...night and day difference. That's a part of life I had to accept.

It's important to be aware of our bad habits so we can prevent them and start developing better ones. As I mentioned a little earlier, these bad habits may be addictions, meaningless distractions, procrastination, saying "no" out of fear instead of taking the opportunity, not cutting off people who disrupt your peace, etc. We all have or had certain things we do that initially bring us a good feeling, but then those feelings go away and we are left feeling empty, disappointed, and unhappy. That's exactly what temporary satisfaction is; it feels good for a couple of seconds, minutes, or days, and then that unavoidable feeling of emptiness comes back like it always does. It comes down to how long you want to entertain those feelings for.

For change to start, you must observe and become aware of your bad habits. Then you need to have the desire to change it. And lastly, you need to take action based on your desires. Habits and addictions are hard to let go of, and it is common to fall off occasionally in the beginning stages (as long as you don't give up!). Here are some of the most common addictions that is applicable to both females and males:

- Addiction to drugs

- Addiction to smoking

- Addiction to food

- Addiction to pornography

- Addiction to your phone

- Being overly obsessive in your relationship

A very simple explanation of what addiction is: you know if you are addicted if you can't say no to something or you can't stop yourself from doing it. Every single type of addiction is detrimental to your well-being.

Even though it isn't really "fitting" to talk about, and I really wasn't planning on talking about it, I want to shed some light about pornography because I think it will be of extreme value to many people. It's a little taboo because it's one of those topics, like money, death and God, that people seem to avoid talking about. Porn applies to mainly guys but is, of course, not limited to them, as some girls can deal with an addiction to porn as well. I'm going to go ahead and say this: addiction to porn leads to very damaging consequences whether we are conscious about them or not. And yeah, yeah, I know some people are going to say, "if it doesn't harm anyone then it isn't bad!!" That's a complete lie. You are harming yourself, your soul, the way you view women and men, your future wife or husband, and your relationship with God. Need I say more? What's the opposite of love? Lust. Lust is all that pornography exhibits and encourages.

"For speaking out arrogant words of vanity they entice by fleshly desires, by sensuality, those who barely escape from the ones who live in error, promising them freedom while they themselves are slaves of corruption; for by what a man is overcome, by this he is enslaved" (2 Peter 2:18-19). We think that by engaging in hedonism (the pursuit of pleasure) we free ourselves, but like that quote says, we become slaves to it. Addiction to porn ruins people. It ruins marriages. It ruins love. It robs people of their innocence. It makes us see people as complete objects instead of as God's children or people with value and dignity. It perverts our minds. It makes us blind to how real love is supposed to be. It distorts our image of how women and men are supposed to act with each other. It abuses the innate goodness and unity of sex. The more one watches porn, the more he or she numbs their ability to get stimulated, which also becomes harmful for a future relationship.

There is a reason as to why the Bible mentions it, it isn't just to restrict something upon us. Unlike some people who want to make billions of dollars from people who will fall into the ways of the world, God wants to free us from this which is why we are warned against it. Like I keep mentioning, we were made in love, for love, to give and to receive love. Anything opposite of that will lead us into a dark place. The goal should be to see in the eyes of love, not lust. We need to see people's souls, not just their bodies. We need to ask ourselves, "How can I help that person?" as opposed to "how can I use that person for my personal gain?" There are so many statistics showing how negatively pornography can affect us. Trust has been broken, marriages have ended, and toxic addictions have started.

Another thing to note is that you don't know what goes on in terms of where the women and men are coming from in these videos. You don't know if the woman is being harmed, forced, or trafficked into acting. Maybe there was no consent, it was blackmail, or some other horrible circumstance. In an industry that makes billions of dollars, unjust practices are bound to happen.

We *must* work on our weaknesses. We *must* get to work today. These problems will *not* pass with time, they will only get worse.

You probably understand well now that the path to success and self-mastery is *not* an easy one. There are many bumps along the way, fixed beliefs that need to be changed, and a whole lot of sacrificing done. It truly isn't a path for everyone, but if it is for you, then you must put the necessary effort if you want the outcome.

I care so deeply about other people's issue, and I want to spread awareness in any way that I possibly can. I want to scream and shout that you don't need to compromise anything to get to your dreams. I want to encourage everyone that overcoming your issues is hard, but it is so rewarding and will bring so much satisfaction.

You have a choice, and you can make it today. Right now. Are you willing to leave whatever has been holding you back for a long time and join the path to success?

Chapter 15

Mastering Your Mind

"You are the master of your destiny. You can influence, direct and control your own environment. You can make your life what you want it to be."

--Napoleon Hill

In Napoleon Hill's books, he often talks about how successful people have the ability to control their minds. Sounds kind of "witchcrafty" and "too good to be true", but it isn't at all. In other words, it means having an extremely high sense of discipline. A simple, yet highly pivotal point that Hill writes in his book, *Think and Grow Rich,* is that "You either control your mind or it controls you. There is no halfway compromise." Agreed. You can't be half pregnant! There is absolutely no compromise. Mind control is not an "I will practice this when I feel like it" type of thing, but it is an everyday grind that will bring an abundance of rewards, including success and prosperity.

Personally, I have not mastered this fully, because I only started working on a harder level of discipline about a year ago, but I have improved significantly and remarkably. I have improved to the point where I am the total opposite of who I was last year, and even half a year ago. I am constantly working on my mental game, leaving my bad habits behind, learning, changing and growing. I am striving for success!

The best thing about mind control is that every single person is capable of doing it. It is not a privilege to those who have more opportunities and more money, or an impossibility to those who are less fortunate and don't have much to start with. There is no bias and no requirement because it is all mental. Everyone has a mind. The only difference between my "success" and your success is how we use our minds. The only influence I can think of is what type of environment we were raised in. Did you grow up in poverty? Are your parents typically pessimistic? Or optimistic? Did your parents spoil you? Many of these things influence the way we think and act, but fortunately, our minds can be changed through repetition and a different pair of eyes to look from (change of perception).

Our minds form a perception, which manifests into our day to day lives. It is as simple as this: if your perception of the world is negative, then you are going to be a negative person. If your perception of the world is positive, then you are going to be a positive and optimistic person. We can use the glass half empty or half full analogy with this because it is our views that determine our way of thinking, so to speak. Our way of thinking will determine how we behave, act, and especially how we feel.

Not only do we need a great amount of discipline, but we also need a definite plan in life. We need to know what we are going to do, what we want to attain, and how we are going to do it. Success does not sync with "going with the flow" because the flow will end up hitting a dead end. Many young adults either get frustrated or give up because they don't have the slightest clue of what they want to do, but they don't actually put the effort into finding it. I have talked to many college students who have said that they are majoring in this and that, and when I asked what they want to do with their degree, all of them said they don't know. So, this will essentially be going through the motions without a plan. Who else does this?

Do we not see an issue here? There was one young woman who told me she is majoring in Political Science, doesn't really know what to do after college, and that she took a semester off to "find herself." I asked her what she did during that break, and she said that she went to work, concerts and overall had "fun." At this point, I was really shocked with how many college students don't know what they want to do after they graduate or if they even care about what they are studying. And like I said, I think that's fine. It's just when most people say they "want to find" themselves, what they actually do is put that off and hide it with "fun" and busy work. Or some people's hearts tell them that they really aren't passionate about what they're studying, but they stick with it for a number of reasons. There's a bunch of reasons that stem from fear. Wanting to please your parents because you fear their disapproval, having the fear of going into the unknown so you hold on to what you're comfortable with, feeling so much self-doubt that it overcomes your desires, and so on. As a result, they spend their days filling it with aimless entertainment to compensate.

It has become so normalized in our culture, and it helps nobody except the people who want to "go with the flow," because it gives them an excuse not to have a purpose. It is normalized to spend all four years of college doing what most students do and then miraculously know what you want to do after graduation. It is normalized to do the absolute bare minimum for your self-development. It is normalized to oversleep and under sleep. It is normalized to be average and mediocre. Just look around your friend circle and other people who you surround yourself with.

I assume that you picked this book up because you want to change. Well, today is the day to try something new or do something you have always wanted to do for yourself. When I put out my very first YouTube video, I had absolutely no intention of being in the place I am now. I loved being in front of the camera and producing content, so I just stuck with it. You seriously don't know what the result will be until you try and keep trying. Do something that genuinely makes you happy because if you have no sparkle in your eyes for your work, then there will always be someone who will work harder and do it better than you.

Mastering your mind takes a lot of dedicated work every single day.

The more you apply yourself to forming better habits, the easier it will get for you to adapt to another new thing you want to take on later. Taking the very first step towards change and then keeping up with it is always the hardest part, but when you overcome both of those, you will become unstoppable. After all, mastering self-discipline comes from controlling your habits and habits are made through persistent effort and commitment. My desire to achieve a successful early morning routine meant that I had to begin waking up before the sun rose almost every day. My obsession for becoming more fit meant that I had to eat better foods and exercise almost daily. My overall hunger for success meant that I had to take *all* of the necessary steps, sacrifice anything holding me back, and constantly reposition my mind to feel discomfort so I could keep pushing forward. Through this, I self-transformed from dust to discipline.

Chapter 16

Success Formula

"Success comes to those who become success conscious."
--Napoleon Hill

I love that quote from Napoleon Hill. Being "success conscious" means surrounding yourself around success and being fully aware of it mentally. When I said "I had to take *all* of the necessary steps" in the last few sentences of the last chapter, this comes into play. Yeah, it's easy to want success, but to *really, really* want success is a much different story. For me, the hardest part was battling the deeply rooted insecurity I had of not being good enough. "Am I really capable of writing a book?" "Am I really good and smart enough to start a business that will compete with some of the best apps out there?" "Can I really step in front of an audience and talk to them?" This. Thankfully, I have read many books and and followed or watched some of the greatest people in this world to know that it's all possible. By reading Hill's books, I became convinced that the only limitations I had was set up in my mind. It's a mental game.

I began following a ton of people who were successful and who inspired me. Some of those people include Gary Vaynerchuk, Oprah, Grant Cardone, Mel Robbins, David Goggins, Rachel Hollis and more. I began watching YouTube videos from Bill Gates, Elon Musk, and some of the others I mentioned as well. Anything to consume content from the best of the best and see how they think, speak, and execute. This is what it means to become success conscious. On top of that, it takes a lot of mental work by visualizing and manifesting. I naturally visualize and "fake interview" myself with the strong belief that one day I will get to the exact place I am seeing myself be in my mind. Recently, I have started incorporating this in the morning and at night because I realized that I was getting a bit discouraged since I have no fruits of labor to enjoy yet. I am in the "grind" process where I don't see any results thus far, so this will keep me feeling optimistic and faithful.

The more you talk about it, the more you will feel it within every bone of your body. The more you tell yourself, "I will do this. God has my back. I will overcome anything standing in my way," the more you will also believe in yourself and execute. The Law of Attraction is essentially a process of manifestation and it is very much real. Either good or bad, what you focus your mind on you will bring into reality. To even get to this place, you have to have a big desire in whatever you want to accomplish.

If you have no feelings attached when you get in the zone of visualization, belief, and meditation, it won't work.

I think that faith plays a significant role as well. When I was younger, I always had this sense of security that no matter what could've went wrong, I would've been fine. I always knew that if I hypothetically lost my money, embarrassed myself publicly, or anything else that could go wrong, I knew that it was temporary. Now, I have the same thing in addition with fully trusting God. I have total faith in God, and I trust His plan for me. If something isn't happening that I want to happen, fine, that isn't up to me when God delivers certain situations or people in my life. As long as I do my part, that's all I can really do. Whether it's with my career, future relationship, finance, or an experience, I know that whatever is coming has a meaningful purpose.

I often see many people misinterpret trusting God as having the person sit back and wait for miracles to fall down on his or her lap. We shouldn't think that way. First and foremost, I think most people already block off many of these blessings by their way of thinking in the first place. Again, Law of Attraction: what you think will manifest. If you appreciate God's goodness and are grateful with what's in your life, more blessings will come to you! If you believe that something is impossible to achieve or that you aren't good enough, unworthy, or weak, then you trick your subconscious into thinking that way.

I enjoy this quote from the Bible, and I personally believe it to be true. In Matthew 19:26, "Jesus looked at them and said, "With man this is impossible, but with God all things are possible."" In certain aspects, I really do think we are limited in many ways and to achieve something that is extremely hard or "impossible," you would need to access it spiritually.   God gives us that special type of strength to overcome anything. Keep that in mind.

However, you don't have to be religious or spiritual to have confidence in yourself and in what you do in what you do. You want to create a business? Have faith that you will persevere and get through it. You want to do anything that takes stepping out of your comfort zone? Believe that you can do it and will do it. Having faith and discipline are similar in the sense that if you have both of these it can prevent you from giving up.

Some people carry around their own success formula, I happen to have one too! Aside from the four bodies, I believe you have to have these four things in order to propel yourself to success:

The 3 D's + Faith

Dedication + Determination + Discipline x Faith = Greatness Achieved

It's quite a simple formula, and it's very easy to remember. We just talked about faith, so I'll break down the other three.

Dedication: You must be dedicated to what you do. This means you put in the work. Not once or twice a week, but around six to seven times a week. Dedication is effort, and without effort, the success formula will not work. My first form of dedication that I remember vividly was when I started getting into fitness. Nobody could've stopped me, and I rarely took a rest day because I was so hungry for the results. You must stay loyal to your goals, this is called dedication.

Determination: Similar to the first one, yet a bit different. You must be determined with what you want to accomplish. This means that your eyes are on the prize; it relates to the phrase "I can and will do it." No matter what happens, you will achieve your goal. I was determined to never delete my YouTube channel, even when my classmates from sophomore year found out and began making fun of my videos. I promised myself that I wouldn't stop making them. Without determination, the success formula will fail.

Discipline: 100% all in the mind. You must be disciplined to stick with your goals, even when things get tough, as they always will. This is when your life seems to be taking a downward spiral or motivation takes a rest day, but your discipline will not falter to this. The hardest days are when our character is built. Yes, I did not want to go to the gym. Yes, I did not want to work on my project. Yes, I wanted to do less and give less. And yes, I am human and have faced temporary defeat here and there. No matter what, I still kept pushing and if I fell, I would rise up again. Without discipline, the success formula will never work.

Now, don't be afraid if all of this starts scaring you and your mind starts telling you that you will never be great, you will never "make it," and that you don't have what it takes to succeed. I thought like this almost all of my life because I never had confidence instilled in me. There's something in us that loves making us feel weak and reluctant which is why having faith in ourselves and in God (if you choose to believe in Him) is crucial.

The greatest thing about this formula is that it can be taught and instilled to anyone who is willing to accept it. As I mentioned before, all good things in life take some time and work to show themselves. It took me constant trial and error, but everything kept getting better because of the mental fortitude I was building. The more I put in effort into things that matter most to me today, the more tomorrow becomes a little easier. I don't take much time to force myself to do the most difficult tasks compared to what I would do before. Instead of spending long minutes or hours thinking about it, I do it now.

Stay true to yourself. Just because we now see many people have their own business or certain stream of income doesn't mean that it's for you. We all have our own path to be on, so because somebody else's path might look shiny and glorious for now, doesn't mean that you should emulate it. Be authentic and make sure to set a proper intention with everything that you do. Stand out from the crowd to create a unique and authentic voice for yourself. Within certain industries, it feels like everyone and their mother sounds the same, posts the same, and communicates the same. Don't be afraid to show who you really are every single day no matter who you may be meeting. Real people want to see the real you.

Long-term growth over short-term growth. Lots of people want to become one hit wonders or get overnight success, but rarely does that actually happen and the chances of that being temporary is high. If you want to make a life-long impact, then that's done in longevity and planning for long-term. The catch is patience. Oh man, God certainly taught me a lot about patience. We naturally want overnight success, that stroke of luck, which was something that was constantly running through my mind years ago. I accepted that this wasn't going to be my fate and that I would actually have to work hard and smart if I wanted to come close to becoming successful. Nobody was going to help me. Fortunately, I have come to appreciate the journey because of how much patience and discipline I was and am gaining.

Dedication, determination, discipline and faith will get us far in life. Through daily application and effort, we can master this formula. Let's go!

Chapter 17

Success Requires Sacrifice

"I want to be in the arena. I want to be brave with my life. And when we make the choice to dare greatly, we sign up to get our asses kicked. We can choose courage, or we can choose comfort, but we can't have both. Not at the same time."
--Brené Brown

I've already touched up on this in past chapters, but I thought it would be even more beneficial if talked about extensively.

Sacrifices have to be made if we want to become better individuals and join the journey to success, it is inevitable. The first step is to gain awareness of your "dark" side, the side that has bad habits, thoughts, and actions. These things that are hindering you from becoming your best self should be gradually worked on until they are put to waste. I think of it similar to hauling garbage around. One by one, you put garbage into the garbage can, and then you throw it all away in a dumpster, and voila! You will eventually become lightweight, able to move freely in whichever direction you want. When this happens, your mind opens up and becomes clean, new and ready for positive thoughts, miracles and growth!

I have sacrificed many things to get closer to my fullest potential, here are some of the things:

- I sacrificed sleeping in. I now go to bed at around 9:30, so I am properly rested for an early rise of 5:20 am. Rise and grind baby!

- I sacrificed temporary disconnection between my parents and I because I wanted to go a direction that would make me happy even though it was different from the traditional path (school, college, then job) my parents expected me to take. This resulted in a temporary "disappointment" for my family.

- I sacrificed the life of mediocrity when I decided that I wanted to achieve great things and overcome all mental barriers. I chose to break free from the barriers either me or the people around me have set. I wanted to achieve *my* fullest potential.

- I temporarily sacrificed romantic affiliations with men and have turned a blind eye to it. This essentially means that I don't entertain other people because I may get "lonely" or have the desire for "having someone there." I made a choice to never settle again, and I am fully aware that finding a man that embodies all that I embody is rare. We are Queens, and we deserve a King that will support and join our Empire. Nothing less!

- I sacrificed entertainment to avoid wasting time. Anything that doesn't benefit my mind, body, or soul is considered meaningless to me. Watching Netflix when needing to get my tasks done was not an option. That's how much I value my time.

- I sacrificed putting my time and energy into anything or anyone that would hold me back from becoming a better person, whether it be friends, men, or any other various activities.

- I sacrificed the "going out" and party mentality. I stay at home on weekend nights. It just wasn't for me, and it didn't make me happy.

- I sacrificed "hanging out" with people. This doesn't mean that I have completely became an isolated hermit because that would actually make me unhappy, but for majority of the time, I am alone. The only friendship I crave is to have a Mastermind group. How nice would it be to gather in a coffee shop with freshly brewed coffee in our hands and talk about business, philosophy, and our goals? That is my type of fun. A group or best friend that elevates and inspires you, what a dream. Being on the path to success is a very lonely climb, but I would rather be doing what I do now compared to what I used to do in the past.

- I sacrificed tradition. I chose to do things my way no matter what other people might've thought or said of me. I didn't want to be put in a box and get told "this is what you should be doing for someone your age." That isn't going to get me anywhere!

- I sacrificed a weak mentality that was engrained in me from childhood. I was surrounded by people who told me "no," "you will fail," and "there's nothing special about you." I battled it often throughout High School, and I eventually came to a point in 2019 when I threw in the towel and called BS on all of it. I was done selling myself short, it was time for me to reach for the moon.

- Ultimately, and most importantly, I sacrificed my old self to be in union with God. My sinful habits and behaviors all had to be washed away because of my realization that "my kingdom is not of this world," it is in Heaven. I want to be good to God, I want to do His will, and I want to love and respect Him just as He does to me except tenfold. Of course, there will be times when I sin by doing or saying something I shouldn't, but I pick myself up as soon as possible because I am human and make mistakes. And because my mistakes are made in the past and I don't choose to hold them against myself, I forgive myself. Whenever I make a mortal sin, I go to Confession (or Reconciliation) as soon as I can to get it off my conscience and properly ask God for forgiveness. It's basically like free therapy!

This is the life I chose. Some people might think this is "way too much," but it really is what it is. I'm not lying, bragging, or over-exaggerating. *This* life makes me so happy and fulfilled. Within any second, I can make a decision to go back to college, surround myself around drama and gossip, and go out with people. I can throw in the towel *easily*. This type of lifestyle will *always* be waiting and won't be leaving. But for now, I am following where my heart is leading me towards.

Like I've said multiple times, we are all called on a different path. Yours isn't going to be like mine, and mine isn't going to be like yours naturally. I'm just a simple girl with a drive, that's really it. But, if you choose to read this book and say, "I want that, she inspires me," then all props to you. I'll see you at the top!

When I found out that I got cheated on, I was overcome by anxiety, but I simultaneously knew that this would also set me free. I was free because I knew I would never go back to that emotionally and verbally abusive relationship ever again. I also gradually cut off any friends that didn't motivate or inspire me. Why waste our time on people who don't bring anything good to the table? I had to move out of my parents' house and find an apartment because I couldn't take the negative environment anymore. I needed a space where I could fully be myself without being bothered or feel like I am causing a burden on someone else. I needed just *me* time.

Here's a wonderful and inspirational quote that I picked up from the book *Three Feet from Gold* by Sharon Lechter and Greg Reid, "The person you will be in 5 years is based on the books you read and the people you surround yourself with today." Based off of the massive growth I have made within a short amount of time, I would even shorten this time period to a couple of months or even half a year.

The people who you surround yourself with is game-changing. People do give off different types of energies, or what some people can also call, "vibes." We have probably heard of someone using the phrase, "she/he gives off a bad/good vibe." This is exactly what I'm talking about. That being said, we should be mindful of the people we talk to or hang out with because they will either influence us or at least give off their energy, whether it be a positive or a negative force. There have been many times when I hung out with people and didn't feel good afterward. There also have been times when I've felt my spirit elevate and a great sense of joy and peace would fill my body. Do not ignore the signs your body tells you. If you feel anxiety, worry, and sadness, then that should indicate to you that you probably shouldn't be surrounding yourself with these people. There's nothing wrong with that. Become aware and use your intuition, it will guide you to what feels right or wrong.

I learned that if you even have to ask yourself questions stemmed from doubt like, "Is this person really the one?" Or "Would I be better and do better without them?" Then the answer to those are already a "no." This doesn't just apply to relationships, it can be with a friend, a job, or anything else. I mean think about it, you wouldn't even have to question anything if the person was right or genuinely good for you. We don't always have to ask about everything, we can simply quiet down and start *feeling*.

Keep in mind, God doesn't send people in our lives to cause us anxiety, worry, or heartbreak. Do you really think He would want that on you? There's a wonderful man on Instagram that goes by the name Ace Metaphor, and he said in one of his videos, "God doesn't want him for your life, Satan does. Satan was the one who sent you that man, and you fell for his temptation. You are the daughter of God, do you think He wants to see you cry? So why would He send you a man that makes you cry?" Wow, the accuracy of that. Ace was specifically talking about men, but his words aren't just limited to that. This can be applied with everything. If you turn a blind eye from what your intuition is trying to tell you, all I have to say is, good luck!

With friends, I've encountered this issue many times. Why hang around people who have no goals and no ambition if you are the polar opposite of that? It doesn't make sense. You should hang out with like-minded people who share your morals and mentality. I don't think that professional athletes hang around high school athletes. I don't think that Bill Gates or Elon Musk spend their time with people who aren't intelligent and driven. There's nothing wrong with these people, it's simply that they aren't at the same level. Why would I spend my time with someone who is unsure of what they are going to do tomorrow when I already have my entire week planned? I won't, because I value myself and my time. Again, I'm *not* saying someone is more inferior or superior over the other not one single bit. I'm just saying that the birds of a feather flock together.

Another thing to be cautious of are people who are better at talking than doing. We all have or had a person like that in our lives who say they are going to do this and that but never do it. You don't want to be associated with these types of people if you want to get to the top. Ambition is wonderful, but ambition that isn't backed by action and result is useless and meaningless. What I also see happen most often are all of the goals that people set for themselves but then get put on the back burner usually resulting from a new relationship. That other person starts becoming a priority instead of their own selves. You can still be in a healthy relationship and work on becoming your best self.

Like I've said before, it's completely okay to cut people off who aren't doing you well, have your best interests at heart, or who you have simply outgrown. I would much rather prefer being alone than to hang out with people who bring nothing to the table.

Success takes sacrifice, and it is up to you what you want to "give up." Dave Ramsey said, "The most important decision about your goals is not what you're willing to do to achieve them, but what you are willing to give up." Remember that garbage example I used? I believe that we need to throw away that garbage first before we start planning moves for how we will become successful or whatever it is we want to do in life. Remember when I said that throughout my high school years, I tried to reconnect with God but couldn't do it fully? That's because I was still holding onto my toxic life of sin. When I made a commitment to let all of that go that one summer, it made all of the difference in the world, and I began to work on my relationship with God. It was unlike anything I have ever experienced. Find what and who you need to let go off and do it. Choose yourself, you deserve it.

Chapter 18

Making Money Moves

"Financial freedom is a mental, emotional and educational process."
--Robert Kiyosaki

Most of us, if not all of us, want to make money. Money gives support, comfort, and the increase of opportunity. It can also be quite the opposite and turn from good to bad, depending on how we view and use money. I have personally seen and experienced both sides of this. One can be liberating, and one can make you feel like a slave. It is extremely important that we change our perception on money if it's the second type.

A wonderful book on finance that I recommend everyone to read is, *Rich Dad Poor Dad,* by Robert Kiyosaki. He talks about the importance of having financial freedom, which essentially means having enough money (mainly passive income) to afford the type of lifestyle we want. Financial freedom means not having to live paycheck to paycheck and constantly worry about the next day, which a majority of people do. He put it perfectly by saying that our educational system teaches us how to get jobs instead of how to make money.

Years of schooling and 5-6 figures in tuition spent just to (maybe) get a job that might not even guarantee financial security. The only class my High School offered that taught about money was Economics, and even that was only a semester class. We learned about the debt college students get themselves into, some technical Economics terms, and the rest that I don't quite remember. I do, however, remember that we had a project where we had to start our own business (this was helpful to an extent) and last but certainly not least, we watched Shark Tank. That's such a great show.

Money is obviously important. It shouldn't be put on a pedestal, but I believe we all can agree that we would rather be financially comfortable than be poor. Therefore, it is of great value to learn about finance and how to properly manage money, so we avoid blowing it on either the next shiny thing or something that inflates the ego. But don't get me wrong, it's great to buy something that makes you feel good, but there should be a healthy balance to it. Partially with what I am saying is that you don't want to base your worth off of the things you have because that's most definitely the wrong place to start.

Earlier this year, I kept saving, saving, and saving just to look at a pretty number in the bank account. This was stupid of me to do. It looked nice, but nice wasn't going to improve my brand and business. The money was stagnant and not being allocated anywhere. I realized that I needed to stop thinking short-term and begin to invest more into my business and other forms of investments.

When I was around 18 years old, I began splurging high amounts on fine jewelry. It's like I would go into a jewelry store and felt that I *had* to buy something. It was exactly what I said a few sentences ago, ego inflation. "Oh! I am wearing thousands of dollars on me; I feel *so* good." I felt different if I didn't wear my jewelry, incomplete so to say. By "different," I meant that I felt like my value diminished a little. This, my friends, is called an attachment.

Cutting off my attachment to materialistic possessions felt and still feels great. Once put into the right perspective, these are items that don't *really* do anything for us. They don't propel us to become better and kinder individuals, nor do they make us more centered or at peace. Like I said before, these things come internally. However, there is absolutely nothing wrong with treating yourself if that's what your heart desires. We also have to keep in mind of our financial goals, can you really afford that? Maybe it isn't even about the money, think if whatever you're about to buy is going to make you into a better you. Would it be worth it in the long run? Think both short term and long term.

If we want to see more money, we need to spend less and invest more. Investing can be in the form of real estate and stocks, but there are many more. These are just the two I personally know. Setting all excuses outside, how you choose to prioritize your income is all on you. You are accountable. If you continue to spend your money recklessly without looking into how you can save and invest properly, that's on you. Nobody else to blame!

We all know the trends on platforms like Instagram. The more you flex, the "cooler" you appear. We see teenagers with BMW's, famous people on private jets, Louis Vuitton this and Gucci that. Now, there is absolutely nothing intrinsically wrong with this. We only get to that when we start thinking, "I have to have that in order for people to like me or perceive me as being cool." Some people's goals change into, "I am going to become a millionaire just so that I can buy anything I want to." That's when the chase for money begins and before you know it you have lost your authenticity.

Self-confidence and acceptance are what we need more of in our lives. We are sometimes so bothered by other people's lives that we forget to live our own! There's been so many times when I have seen a celebrity, famous person, or an influencer with much more than me. On top of that, it even looked like they gained everything much quicker than I did. And then I get disheartened. "Why haven't I received the fruits of my labor yet?" "They can do this, but I can't?" I know that I am not the only one who went through this, probably everybody reading this right now felt the same way at certain points of their lives.

I've learned a significant lesson by going through this. I constantly have to remind myself that I am on my own path and nobody is going to walk it for me. I'm moving in my own lane and at my own speed. You know, I've noticed that throughout my entire adolescence, God kept and keeps trying to teach me patience. My desires weren't going to come overnight, not even after a couple of years. I am extremely grateful for that because I can focus on becoming my strongest, best, and most disciplined self in the meantime. I want to work hard for it, so that the victory can taste even sweeter and more rewarding. 1 year, 5 years, 10 years…bring it on.

A common misconception is thinking that having more money or fame will solve all of our problems. More likely than not, it adds to problems if only we have the wrong perception or lack financial literacy. There is a reason as to why lottery winners become broke again. There is a reason as to why getting a higher paycheck may result in worse spending tendencies. The more money we make, the more our horizons expand. We start seeing all of the things we can now afford, and we start indulging. Then, we have to force ourselves to check our bank accounts and see that we don't have that much left

177

anymore. This is a common cycle with young adults, and it's a poor mindset to have.

Let's discuss more of what we see online, the wealth flooding from all sorts of personalities and public figures. Unfortunately, many of these people are actually bombarded with problems, mental issues for the most part. One may ask, "Nastassia, how could such people possibly have mental health problems if they have everything they want?" Great question! First off, we shouldn't assume, seriously. We absolutely have no *real* clue what is really going on in any person's life. Yes, that does include Kylie Jenner.

Since these people are constantly in the eyes of the public, many of them have to maintain an image. People maintain images to distort other people from actually seeing the reality as well as to please other people's views. In other words, they are putting up a front. Everyone seems to want to be the "next best thing," so comparing yourself to another person also gets thrown in the mix. It becomes a space of insecurity as opposed to something that should be used in a beneficial way. I really do believe that the world would be a better place if people used their platform to spread awareness and create change in whatever they feel most passionate about.

This is why accepting and loving ourselves is necessary, because if we don't, then we welcome a life of insecurities which further leads to mental health problems and other negative consequences. Just to give an example.

This obviously doesn't just happen to these certain types of people; this happens to the vast majority. So please, be aware and learn not to compare yourself to anyone, especially not celebrities. The second anyone begins this process they have wasted their time that could never be brought back. Time that could've been spent productively on something else.

Another common misconception I see happening often is misjudging and stereotyping wealthy people as greedy, scammers, and egocentric. I was raised by people who thought this way too. There are even some people who go to great length to despise wealthy people simply because they are wealthy. Like I said, it speaks more about you than it does about them!

I felt the need to address this topic simply to get the point across that many of these people really do meaningful and charitable work with their money. They might just do it silently. With a great amount of money comes a great amount of potential power that could be used in many amazing ways. It's better for us not to judge people who we don't even know, and people we may even know too! As humans, we always make mistakes, have things in our lives we need to improve on, and things that we cannot control happens to us. It is better to just not judge or assume. Not to mention, it's a waste of time!

All of that being said, be wise with your money and take the time to learn more about it because we definitely do not get taught about it in school. Might as well learn about it as early as possible so that you will have the rest of your life properly financially set!

Chapter 19

Not Every Day Will Be Your Best Day

"Your best is going to change from moment to moment; it will be different when you are healthy as opposed to sick. Under any circumstance, simply do your best, and you will avoid self-judgment, self-abuse and regret."
--Don Miguel Ruiz

There are two different coping mechanisms for having off days depending on how you judge yourself. The first way is acknowledging what went wrong, not taking it too seriously, and then trying to do better the next day. This is constructive. The destructive way would be to harshly criticize yourself and feed your head with judgement and self-doubt. As human beings, oh we love doing that. Coming from experience, I've learned that this way of thinking does absolutely nothing except produce negativity. Instead of getting down on ourselves about something we did or didn't do in the past (even if it's 30 minutes ago), we try to do better and improve next time.

We can't control the past because it's over. In this chapter, you will learn how to think more constructively and positively.

I used to be an absolute pro at being my harshest critic, until I came to realize that I'm wasting my time thinking those thoughts anyway. The thought process went like, "I did not work hard enough today which turns into "I was not good enough today... I need to do more" and on it goes. Why am I complaining about something I can fix and improve on? It was important for me to become aware of this and change it immediately. Sometimes, yeah, we can give a little more effort. If that is the case, then give more effort. It is as simple as that, yet our minds can make everything so complicated. Work through it, do a little more tomorrow than you did yesterday. Do more reps, pray a little longer, and start doing things that are uncomfortable for you to do. If you do this every day, the amount of progress you will make in half a year to a year will be tremendous. The little steps add up! To summarize, don't waste time complaining or judging yourself over something you can always improve on the next day. Let it go, restructure your thoughts, create a game plan and execute.

We can't make every day be the top "best" day. Life can be predictable, but at some points it can't be. Things we cannot control may come up, we get sick, or we might accidentally indulge in something we shouldn't have.

Regret might come up, and then the self-hate starts. We tend to put too much pressure on ourselves which of course, results in unhappiness. The key here is not to dwell too much on things. Sacrificing your peace over something that you won't care much about in a couple of days or a couple of months isn't worth it. I've experienced this so much with the people around me. When you start becoming more aware of everything, you begin to realize how insignificant other people's dramas really are. Something that could be solved in seconds gets prolonged to unnecessary lengths.

In Don Miguel Ruiz's book, *The 4 Agreements*, his last agreement is "always do your best." He says, "When you wake up refreshed and energized in the morning, your best will be better than when you are tired at night. Your best will be different when you are healthy as opposed to sick; it will depend on whether you are feeling wonderful and happy, or angry and upset." This is very true. We all have different ways of doing our best, especially when we have our bad days. Whenever we get in the mode of criticizing ourselves, we need to become aware of this damaging behavior and stop ourselves from slipping into it. In order for us to make tomorrow better than yesterday, we can't just say we will without any feeling. We've all done that "I swear to myself I will do it tomorrow" and then never end up doing it. You have to put a strong desire behind your words. Do you *really* want to change or improve? Or are you just kidding yourself? Remember, we need to become aware of what we did or didn't do that we may not have liked. Be smart with yourself, otherwise you'll fall into the same patterns you always do. By the way, check out that book! It's a phenomenal read. Don Miguel Ruiz is a stellar writer.

When I was reading the *Miracle Morning* by Hal Elrod, he talked a little bit about high achievers. He says that the difference between them and the *highest* of achievers is that they "are exceedingly grateful for what they have, regularly acknowledge themselves for what they've accomplished, and are always at peace with where they are in their lives." I read that part at a time in my life when I still struggled with patience and gratitude. I thought that this feeling was something that most people who are either on the path to success or are already there regularly go through. That's probably true, but it still wasn't the life I wanted to live. I wanted to strive for success while still being full of love, gratitude and peace. I didn't want my mind to tell me that I wasn't good enough or not doing enough. Therefore, I worked on that and still continue to do so. Things are *bound* to not go my way all the time. There *will* be failure and mistakes. I choose to still remain in love, gratitude and peace because I know that even though it might temporary hurt, there is always someone else going through something worse. You have to keep things into perspective.

With all of that being said, God thankfully gives us many chances to make things right with ourselves, so if we wanted to, we could snap out of our bad mood within seconds. It's all in the mind. It's crucial to prevent that negative mindset from creeping in. Here are some simple steps to follow:

1. Start catching yourself whenever you judge yourself.

2. Give thanks. Say or think of some things you are really grateful for. Make them simple (e.i, your breath, body, heart, shelter, food). Even the fact that you are probably doing much better than billions of other people in the world.

3. Do not focus on what you did in the past. It is right now that matters. You can either dwell on it, or you can get up and try again. Your choice.

4. Think positive. I always say things like, "today will be MY day," "I will have a killer week," "I am capable of doing anything I set my mind to," or just as simple as "I got this." You have to give yourself a pep talk sometimes. Nobody else will do it for you, for free at least.

We may feel on top of the world for a couple of minutes or hours, and then our doubts and insecurities start creeping in, which is why we should follow the steps above. Every single day. A negative thought comes up? Deal with it in a healthy way. There's just this thing in us that wants to make us fearful, and it is truly hard to get out of without the proper mindset, especially if we had a lot of traumatic experiences that resulted in this way of thinking. Trust me, I know. But it's okay because it is something that can most definitely be worked on. I believe that mental health is a priority, which is probably something you haven't learned much in school about. It is more important than studying for a test or finishing some homework up. You know why? Tests are short-term but mental health is long-term. Tests don't determine your life or success, but your mental health determines the outcome of your emotional state which then manifests into everyday life. If you keep piling tasks on top of your exhausted self, your issues are *never* going to go away. We are good at doing this — creating distractions. Time won't heal it either, but it will make it temporary go away. Everyone seems to be okay with temporary until the issues creep up again. Then it's like, "what the heck! Why isn't this going away?" Because you bought into the lie that time heals things when it's just one part of the equation.

If we keep procrastinating and pushing our most difficult tasks away, we will never get anywhere. We always seem to want nicer things, better bodies, and a bigger paycheck, but we neglect one of the most important things which is our mental and emotional body. Not under my watch! Humans thrive with creativity and movement, and regress with stagnation and laziness. Ask yourself: If not now, then when? Move, move, move!

Back when I was on my emotional rollercoaster from 'finding out my ex-boyfriend cheated on me' stage, it was rough. I used to have bad weeks, then I changed them into bad days, which then led me to bad hours, and now I don't really get bothered anymore. Through creating discipline and instilling gratitude, I can snap myself out of my naturally lazy attitude and remind myself that I do and feel best when I am productive, creative and in my state of peace. One of the best ways we can overcome the darkness and gloominess in our lives is to find our passion and hope. Passion creates meaning and purpose. So many people wake up and begin their usual "go with the flow" routine, wasting away their precious hours with work that is meaningless to them. Not to mention, the snooze button also gets hit which tells your mind subconsciously that your day doesn't really matter all that much. If you didn't know that, well now you know! There is also proven research done about the side effects that hitting the snooze button has on your day.

If you care about social justice issues, then start a campaign or create awareness about it. Maybe start a nonprofit organization. If you like taking pictures, take some photography classes and become a photographer. If you like being in front of the camera, start a YouTube channel. If you have a mind of an entrepreneur, start a business. Move, produce and progress. Again, nobody said that going out of your comfort zone and sticking with it will be easy. It is, in fact, extremely hard to swim against the current and to continue doing so consistently (maybe until you are in Bora Bora, kidding).

Today is a new day. Go and do something you've always wanted to do for yourself or for other people.

Chapter 20

Be Open Minded

"When we respect everybody around us, we are in peace
with everybody around us."
--Don Miguel Ruiz

As we go from children to adolescents to young adults and then to adults, we learn from and are influenced by our family, friends and society. I think we can all agree with this by now, right? Therefore, their ways of thinking and perceiving the world will influence our minds one way or another, whether it be gradual or immediate, good or bad. It just depends on how naive and easily influenced you can be. As children, we are obviously like this and believe everything our parents tell us because...well, they're our parents. Shouldn't we fully trust them and believe everything they say? I thought this was the case, but I came to realize in my late teenage years that adults actually don't know everything, at all. I see parents as just grown-up children with added responsibilities. However we grew up, whether it be positive, negative or both, remember that our parents grew up getting influenced by their parents, culture, and society. They have been taught right from wrong, good from bad, and true from untrue just like us.

Most of us have taken what was said by the closest people in our lives, our friends, and society and have run with it without figuring out what rings true for us without the opinion of others. It creates a comfortable atmosphere for us if we don't think for ourselves, even if it doesn't quite sync with your *real* identity. This may result in becoming close-minded. Not only that though, it can also come from having a lack of understanding, experience and perception which makes us form set in stone beliefs, even if our beliefs are completely illogical. We close any opposing form of thought, which most definitely can close us up from many great opportunities or revelations.

There are many traditional ideas that people believe they should follow for various reasons. For example, there are those who have been raised to not think about the significance of life and just to follow the whole "get good grades, go to college, get a degree, get a job and get married" way of life. There is very limited creativity in this, and results in the lack of meaning and depth in one's life. By all means, if you think that this is the right path for you, then go ahead and continue it! But, if this "path" is all you have heard in your life as the "right thing to do," then I highly recommend for you to take a step back, think on your own, and reassess what it is that you really want.

One traditional belief that my family had was that college wasn't an option, it was necessary. Here comes Nastassia, the only person in the family who has absolutely no desire to attend college. I certainly did have opposition, even to the extent of my mother saying that I wouldn't be welcome at my parents' house anymore if I didn't go. This did hurt my relationship with my family, but like I said before, I was not going to sacrifice my happiness to please someone else's set beliefs on how I should live *my* life. Here we see the consequence of the parent to child relationship being compromised from close-mindedness. It isn't right and it isn't fair.

It definitely is not easy breaking out of a mindset that has been instilled for generations or by our parents. It also certainly is not easy living in fear because you don't want to disappoint your family. Ask yourself: would I rather sacrifice my happiness for the sake of others, or would I rather *temporary* sacrifice the happiness of others, not grow in resent with them, and become happy at what I like doing best? The second route is the hardest, but like everything else that is difficult, it will be the most fulfilling and rewarding.

It takes a certain level of awareness to break out of set ways of thinking, if that is what we choose to fix in our lives. I do not know of any people with an entrepreneur-like mindset in my family, so I was definitely the "odd one" one out of everyone, which caused me to have many disagreements with my parents. And being a girl that was extremely obsessed with working out? My parents thought I set myself up for massive failure. I made it quite clear that I cared more for working out than I did for doing my homework, but I also made it clear that I had confidence in myself to become successful. I wasn't really sure how to do that being around 17-18 years old, but I knew that I would figure it out as I go, learn and grow. Saying this seemed to trigger my parents' negativity. "You aren't anything special, you are an average person." *No,* I refused to believe that. It wasn't true.

Around my junior year of high school is when I began wondering what I would study in college. I was absolutely clueless on what I wanted to major in. I asked my parents what they thought, and they predicted that a subject like marketing would be good for me. At that time, I was absolutely positive that I was going to college because I honestly was close-minded and influenced by my environment. Everybody at my school went to college, some even went to Ivy League schools. Ironically enough, I thought dropping out of college was for people who are either lost, dealing drugs, or complete failures in life. I had such a fixed perception because of what my parents, school and society taught me. When senior year came around, I wanted to major in entrepreneurship, knowing that this was as close of a class that resonates with me can get. I applied to more UC's than CSU's (California State

University) because that wasn't really what the students at my school did. It was all about prestige, and the more expensive the school, the more your ego prospers!

Funny enough, I got rejected from all of the UC's I applied to even with a higher SAT score. I'm not sure I would be where I am now if I got accepted into a UC, so I am very thankful for getting rejected. Anyway, I enrolled in the local state university, and about a month before school began, I started my first business, Nasty Fit.

Because I find my dropping out story funny, I'll quickly share it with you. I thought school started on Wednesday instead of a Tuesday. After accidentally going to the wrong classes on the first two days, I finally went to the right business class on the third day. The teacher was talking about the qualities of a leader. I paid attention for about 20 minutes and then I pulled out my notebook and began writing down some business ideas for Nasty Fit. I remember having such a weird feeling from just the idea of "being back at school." It felt exactly like high school except with older students who had more freedom. It didn't feel right at all.

The day after that, I had an Economics class in the morning and an English class in the late afternoon. I was already contemplating skipping the late afternoon class because I wanted to train my lower body. As I was driving to my Economics class, I started getting a craving for Indian food. I had to make a choice within a minute. Do I go to class or do I go get my beloved Indian food? The debate was on.

My desire for Indian food won, so I turned my car around to go back home...the rest was truly history.

Everyone has their own path in life and are on their own journey. My path is different than yours and yours is different from mine. If everyone understood this very simple and obvious concept, it would be so much easier for everyone to be happier and get along better.

Let's take a different approach from being close-minded. Sharing something that is known as "taboo," creates vulnerability and opens you up to harsh disapproval from others. Big deal. By being open, you uncover that protective shield you created by steering away from anything controversial. When people keep certain things to themselves even though they want to share it, more often than not, it really creates a lack of authenticity because you aren't showing others who you really are and what you believe in. Social media influencers know very well that when something hits below surface level, there will be overly sensitive people ready to pounce. Be yourself! There will *always* be someone who disagrees with you. There are definitely people who disagree with Oprah, Michelle Obama, etc., but that doesn't dim their light nor stop them from sharing their truth. If you impact more people positively than you do negatively, then that's really what matters.

I also sometimes bring up my religion and spirituality because it's a massive chunk of who I am. People will tell me that I am delusional, brainwashed, that "Catholics are the worst people on earth" and all kinds of stuff. My internal response is, "Okay. As long as I fully know who I am, I will continue to spread that." Sure, these people might use different words to describe their thoughts and feelings, but all of their comments relate to each other. The saddest part is that the people who are making these types of comments are only harming themselves and ultimately, God.

I believe there are several reasons for the root cause of closed-mindedness (in no particular order):

1. Influence from family or friends from an early age which developed into a strong bias into adulthood. For example, a parent making racist comments about a specific race, which then influences that child to grow up and become prejudiced against that certain race.

2. A negative or traumatic experience resulting in shutting oneself from certain topics completely. For example, a person that might've had a negative experience at their Church ultimately caused them to separate themselves from that religion or from God completely.

3. Cultural influence. For example, a certain culture can be completely against homosexuals. Therefore, when a person from this culture comes across a homosexual person, they will discriminate against him or her for no logical reason.

4. Being a narcissist. A typical narcissist thinks they are better than other people and the ideas they have to offer. They also feel the need to control other people.

There are more reasons, but these four are the ones I have seen happen the most. ~~I know that~~ A traumatic experience can create a huge mental barrier, but if we do not work on it then we will never be healed. And I know that one negative experience can ruin the "whole" experience, but this does not mean that the "whole" thing is actually bad. We just choose to make it that way, even though it isn't the truth.

Here's a common example I know most women experience. When I used to surround myself with people who shared other people's life stories and worldly dramas, I would often hear about men being disloyal and cheating here and there and what seems to be everywhere. On top of that, I also have been cheated on, lied to and verbally abused, but I have come to terms with this. My initial reaction was to project my negative experience to all men, but I knew in my heart that this wasn't true. I know that there are men out there (I have some in my life too) who don't cheat and are wonderful husbands/boyfriends to their significant others. We, as emotional beings, also tend to focus on the emotional events that happen around us. We naturally hear about the wrongs of the world as opposed to all of the rights, which might create us to think that everything is unfair, bad, corrupt, etc. This is another lie. Surround yourself with really good people, and you will see the goodness this world offers.

To close off this chapter, I encourage all of you to practice being open. Open to ideas, opportunities, beliefs, challenges, people, relationships, anything really. When someone tells you something that you don't particularly agree with, ask them why they think that way, instead of criticizing them or putting a title on them. I'm not saying you need to agree with what everyone tells you, but you should form your opinion by being rational. Interaction is also important, whether it be in real life or online. The healthier you can interact, the stronger your bond with the other will be.

Learn to understand other people and see what perspective they are coming from. With every comment, opinion, and belief, there is a reasoning that stems from something much, much deeper. The more you understand the people you interact with, the wiser you will become.

Chapter 21

Be the Change You Want to See

"If we could change ourselves, the tendencies in the world would also change. As a man changes his own nature, so does the attitude of the world change towards him... We need not wait to see what others do."
--Gandhi

I had a phase earlier this year when I became fascinated with Elon Musk and his immense level of creativity and intelligence. I started watching some of his interviews on YouTube and came across one that inspired me. He received one question that asked him why he cares about humanity as much as he does, and he bluntly replied saying "someone has to do it." I love that.

That's the problem. Not enough people are "doing it," not enough people are being the change they want to see in the world. I am not at all saying you have to be a motivational speaker, a philanthropist, or an inventor of something that will help change the world because all of us are called to be of use in our own unique way.

When we are born into this world, we are completely clean and pure. We grow into little children, and we do what is fun and embody the phrase "live, laugh, love." But as soon as we start growing up, maturing, getting to know the world, having more freedom and experiencing life, we become blemished by mistakes, hurt, and trauma. The influence of our environment, friends, and family begins to weaken our potential and mental fortitude. Weeks, months and years can go by without any notice of who we really are as individuals. Whether we were comfortable all of our lives or we acted out and rebelled, most of us have never stopped and thought if we were heading to a path of enlightenment or a path to oblivion. I believe this is one of the biggest purposes to life is to of course, walk the path of enlightenment.

1. Become aware of who you are and where your life is at the moment.
2. Ask yourself if you like the person you are this present day.
3. If you don't, you must desire to change yourself.
4. Put the desire into action.

So many of us are so blind, following the guidelines of what we were told to do, say and think our whole lives. And then as we grow older, we instill it into our children, just like our parents did to us. The humblest of parents will tell anyone that they don't have much clue to what they're doing, they are just trying their best like we are. No matter what lie we have been living in, thanks to God, the Truth will always stay true regardless of who you are and what you do…and the "truth will set you free" John 8:31-32.

Fortunately, many people come to a realization that this is not who they want to be, not what they are meant to do. We want to change the feeling of discontent, unfulfillment, and restlessness because I bet that nobody really wants to feel that. Quite often, these little revelations usually happen when someone experiences suffering, but it isn't limited to that. Some people just get tired of their current lives and want change.

This is when progress starts. We begin healing whatever needs to be healed and becoming more loving towards ourselves. Barriers get broken, fear gets overcome, assumptions fade away, and seeing in the eyes of love takes over. Even after all of the dirtiness and corruption that we may see in people, society, the world and even in ourselves, underneath that mess is goodness and hope. Just like how we were born - good, pure, and full of love. Unfortunately, some people never come to this realization in their lives, so they succumb to regret and misery for all eternity. Life becomes a never-ending hell on Earth. The last thing we want is to live with regret. Our time on Earth isn't infinite, and we can't go back in time.

We must have self-awareness of our actions, thoughts and words. We can never alter something without recognizing it fully. A step to doing this is to be really conscious with the way you interact with people and how you go about your day. <u>Be mindful of how you communicate with people you like and even more attentive with the people you aren't so fond of.</u> Are you seeing and treating everyone in the eyes of love? Or do you get easily irritated and angry with certain people? Who is a benefit in your life and who impacts you in a negative way? This may even be your family, and that's totally okay. Not all families are perfect because they have their own unsolved issues. These issues can unfortunately be brought upon their children, but that is okay. Spend less time with them or avoid them completely. Please do not provoke your parents, especially if they tend to get hot-heated.

A couple of months before I turned 19, the environment got very, very toxic. Arguments and negativity everyday...I was so sick and tired of it. Luckily, I had enough money to rent my own apartment, so I did that. It was one of the best decisions I have made in my life. However, I know that most people can't do that right then and there, but there is always something we can do about it. Save, work and don't spend money on dumb stuff. Delete your social media and remove any other time-wasting distractions you may have and fill those hours with work. When you do this, I bet you will save enough money eventually to move.

When we are unhappy and generally frustrated in life, we tend to put the blame on others. We would rather find *anything* else to blame except for ourselves. Most if not all of the time, it actually has to do way more with us than with others. Ask yourself, "Why am I unhappy at this certain moment?" "What triggered this emotion in me?" "Why do I react so fast based on immediate emotion?" Hold yourself accountable.

Like I've been stressing in this book, in order to appear happy and loving on the outside, we first need to work on it on the inside. The older I get, the more I notice how dissatisfied and rude many people are. I notice it when I'm about and about, going anywhere to eat, and especially with employees. Even working more with people for various projects, man, people don't even want to form any connection. Most people don't strike me as friendly, inviting, or lively. When having the pleasure of finding people to hire, I look for efficiency, enthusiasm, professionalism, passion and reliability. Working for someone or not, don't make it be just about the money. Try to form connections and relationships with people, we *need* to spread more kindness to ourselves, each other and the planet.

Some people don't even say "thank you" anymore, what is up with that? I personally hold the door for both genders whenever I can, but some men don't even do that to other women. It blows my mind every single time. Being a genuinely good person has a domino effect, it really does spread from person to person. My favorite person that shares this is…you guessed it…Gary Vaynerchuk. He is one of the best people at it, and he has changed thousands, if not millions of lives. If someone shares their kindness with me, it makes me want to cherish it and expand it out to the world.

Smile at people, open doors for people, admire the beauty of nature, ask people how they are doing, do something nice for your family. I go out to eat often, and I always make an effort to ask the employees how they are doing and *smile* when I do it. I used to feel a bit shy asking people the simple question of "How is your day going so far?" but the more I did it, the easier it became. I even had people thanking me for asking them this because of how much it meant to them. We all go through tough times, it's inevitable. And sometimes, life isn't going as expected. Many of us want to close up and submerge our minds in our problems, but we need to change the narrative. The more we worry or think about our problems, the less energy we have to look up and see what's around us as well as to enjoy the goodness in our lives.

Also, worrying over something that is probably out of our control isn't going to solve anything either. We don't need x amount of money, x amount of friends, a relationship, or a nice car to enjoy what we are already gifted with. Waking up in the morning and being blessed with another day should be enough. It is the simple things in life that are truly the greatest and most important.

We need to be more in tune with our bodies, minds and souls. They speak to us every day, but our heads are always too loud to hear them. That pit in our stomach, the flare of anxiety, the lack of peace…it is our bodies signaling to us that we don't like where we are and what we are doing.

I want to talk about something important that doesn't get brought up often. The phrase, "it doesn't matter what you do, as long as nobody gets hurt." This misconception leads to a very ignorant and unaware lifestyle. The people who live by this phrase are usually too hung up on this excuse to justify for their behavior. They are completely unconscious that they are hurting themselves the most. Let's take a deeper look.

Without getting too technical, smoking does not harm others. Drinking alcohol does not harm others. Self-hate does not harm others. Being addicted to porn does not harm others (I take that back if you have a significant other). Having sex with multiple partners does not harm others. Lying to yourself and other people does not harm others (until the truth comes out). Overindulging in food or purposefully not eating does not harm others. The list goes on.

Okay, if we really want to get technical about it, these examples do harm other people, such as your family and loved ones – sort of contradicting to what I said, but not to a massive extent at all. Your parents want to see you do and be your best, your closest friends should too.

But let's talk about you. You live with yourself every second of the day and you cannot change nor escape that. Many people who live with this lifestyle of "it doesn't matter because it doesn't hurt anyone" do not see that this way of thinking will result in self-inflicted pain physically, emotionally, mentally and spiritually. We need to make ourselves a priority and start caring for ourselves like most of us care for other worldly things that actually have no long-lasting significance. I believe that we are all made in the image and likeness of God, the Creator of everything good in this world. So, if you intoxicate yourself and fill your head with negativity and self-hatred, wouldn't you essentially be dishonoring the body and mind God gave you? Your original state of goodness, purity and love is a direct reflection of who God is. This is actually one of the signs that point to the existence of God, but that's another topic. Why would you go against that and not expect for it to backfire?

So many times, we forget how to love each other so we begin using each other for pleasure and personal gain. Whenever we start chasing short-term satisfactions, we stop living for ourselves and start living according to other people's views on us. We lose our connectedness with God, our spirituality, each other and the beauty all around us. We want to be accepted by society and seen as cool, "in," and like we got it all. We get lost in the world and what it has to offer. We keep trying to add more and more things in our lives without fixing the original issues. Our insecurities create delusion between how we project ourselves and our core essence. It's time to become aware and start changing our behavior and mentality. Humility will get us to great places.

I always had so many questions as to why so many people do the "bad" things they do. Why are people so mean? Why do we always hear about cheating? Scandals? Drama? Abuse? Injustice? Crime? Divorce? Fights? Apart from it being a fact that social media, news channels, gossip sites, etc., constantly air these things because they know it will get attention from the masses, I still didn't get why it was happening on the scale that it was.

I kept thinking precisely about two things: Why the majority of people are known to be "mediocre" and why most people who claim themselves as "Christian," religious, or spiritual, only use that as a title and don't really practice it? I went deeper into it, took away all bias I might've had, and came up with a possible reason for it.

I think it all comes to show how incomplete we are as individuals, so to speak. I mean, we are all humans which automatically means we fall into sin. The problems start arising when we (which is the majority) do not work out our issues or incompleteness, so then these internal battles manifest into all of the problems we hear about and experience in our lives. And this, I think, is the reason we hear about so many corrupt things happening. Our internal problems get exposed eventually through the way we act, communicate, and behave with other people. The insecurities, traumas, fears, wounds and whatever else that most of us have is going unfixed, and therefore this obviously gets put out onto the real world.

I was reading the well-known book by Dale Carnegie, "*How to Win Friends and Influence People*" and he kept stressing how every single person wants to feel important. That if you try to go out of your way to talk to other people with what they are interested in and get to know more about them as opposed to talking about yourself, wow, what a difference it will make. When I listened to Lewis Howes' podcast with Brené Brown, she brought up how her focus was on the Unite the Right Rally in Charlottesville, Virginia. If you haven't heard about it in 2017, I will give a quick recap of what happened. It was a white supremacist and neo-Nazi rally where the protestors chanted racist and anti-Jew hate speech, or slogans. Essentially, these people are stuck in the time of when Hitler was persecuting Jewish people. Neo-Nazis also hate minority groups, homosexuals, and even some Christians. It's difficult for me to comprehend that something like this still happens, but it really does. Brené made a very insightful point by saying that nobody hates just to hate, and that the Charlottesville event rose from the deep-rooted void of not feeling important enough.

Perhaps this is why haters like when you give them a response, why children cry even though nothing is really bothering them, or why the most important word to us is "I." This is many of us want to get heard. Of course, some go to extreme cases about it like the example I mentioned, and others stay quiet and develop the feeling of not being good enough or not having enough value. Nobody wants to feel useless; we all want to feel valued. Just another point to keep in mind of. The solution to this would probably be to fully acknowledge that you have a unique purpose, then find a purpose if you haven't already, and then execute on that purpose effectively.

It is all through unresolved mental and emotional problems, and quite possibly the lack of spiritual guidance and awareness as well. It makes sense, doesn't it?

Nonetheless, there is so much hope for everyone. Some might feel inspired, some might see humanity as a loss, just depends if we see the glass half full or half empty. Humanity isn't a loss because goodness is abundant, and it will always override anything bad. Love will always, always win. Any second of the day, whether it be in tragedy or in joy. We are humans made of love, and we come together as a community in love and connectedness.

Elevate yourself first and then elevate the people around you. See people in the eyes of love, even if they might not see you in that way.

Be the change you want to see in the world. Will you join me in this? Truly?

Chapter 22

Time to Work

"The only person who was going to turn my life around
was me. The only way I could get turned around was to
put myself through the worst things possible that a
human being could ever endure."
--David Goggins

You have learned about many things thus far. My journey of learning and growing began when I was 18, and yours has now too. But only if you want it. Why do I keep stressing the importance of wanting it? The definition of the word 'motivation' is "the general desire or willingness of someone to do something." Key word: desire. Nobody in the world is possible of installing a desire in you with something you really don't want to do. At the end of the day, it's up to you. Here are the three keys to change again:

1. You must become aware of who you are and whether you like it or not. Do not live a mindless life. Are you proud of your words, thoughts and actions? Are you happy? Or are

you wasting your time? Do you even enjoy the life you live?

2. You must have a strong desire to change.
3. Your desires must be converted into actions. Thoughts and desires have no meaning until they manifest themselves into actions.

We all want to become better. We all want to become healthier. We all want to become successful in whatever way we define success. We all want to be happy. We all want peace. We have so many wants but so little do's. In order to break free from mediocrity, we must force and train ourselves to create a mental discipline. There is NO easy way out, and if your mindset is currently set on trying to find a short-cut, I will gladly and honestly say that there is none. It takes dedication, determination, discipline and faith.

Some of you might think, "uh, I don't think I have what it takes" or "uh, I am not sure I am ready." You do have what it takes, and you are ready. You are as ready now as you ever will be. There is *nothing* special about me or my circumstances that got me to where I am now. No luck that magically fell upon me. I came from a regular family and grew up with a regular life. The only thing that I did was follow my heart, forever and always. No matter who said no, told me I can't, or would try to limit me, I wouldn't let them. I am too stubborn for that! If I did that, oh you certainly can too.

If we want to start this process of change, we must first know what it is that we want to achieve or accomplish. We need to have a goal and then formulate a plan around it. Our goals can range from wanting to make tomorrow a better day all the way too wanting to become multi-millionaires or making an impact on the world. Whatever it is, write every single thing down. Before you start, it's time that you be real with yourself. What is it that you REALLY want and are willing to spend many years, if not the rest of your life working towards?

1. What are your passions? What makes you happy?
2. What do you want to accomplish?
3. What do you want to start and what are your reasons for it?
4. What are your ultimate life goals?
5. Who do you want to become?
6. Who inspires you the most?

To be honest, a couple of years ago my original answers to these questions weren't the most fulfilling, and I experienced the consequences firsthand. I wanted status and money. I got some of it and didn't find myself the least bit fulfilled, happy or at peace. Fortunately, I have grown a lot since then and with that comes completely different answers to these questions. Personally, I have a powerful ambition to make a positive impact in our society and bring awareness into people's lives of what is really important. And thinking about that makes me feel really, really good.

I am so thankful that my eyes were opened at an early age, which makes me even more empathetic to young adults because I have been there and done that! I have experienced what you have, and you are definitely not alone.

I went through many things that made me question if there's anything more to life, a deeper purpose. Let me tell you, once I really committed myself to God, I knew I was *never* going back to how I was before Him. It wasn't a good place to be. I realized that so many things were lies and games, distractions from the most meaningful and greatest things this world has to offer.

There was an Instagram post that captured this so well. It said, "When you have the Holy Ghost (Spirit) inside of you:

-Secular Music won't sound the way it used to.

-Certain jokes won't make you laugh like it used to.

-Going to the club won't make you feel "lit" like it used to.

- "Therefore, if any Mann be in Christ, he is a new creature" (2 Corinthians 5:17)."

Amen. Everything becomes different because you *grow*. You grow from the person you used to be.

There is only progress from here. A man named Pierre Teilhard de Chardin said, "We are not human beings having a spiritual experience. We are spiritual beings having a human experience." Personally, I believe we are both, but I understand his point completely. We are not just made of flesh and bone, we are also spiritual beings made for having union with God. Think about it, what do you have to lose?

We will never be free and reach that deep longing in our souls for more if we reject our spiritual body. That being said, be careful about what you set your goals to be. We all know by now that money alone won't fulfill you. Fame won't fulfill you. Overworking yourself won't fulfill you. A new relationship most certainly not fulfill you. Your ego is not YOU; it is a disguise that masks insecurities and promotes an excess of pride. We need to overcome the power our egos have and work on the four bodies: mental, emotional, spiritual, and physical. Robin Sharma, a profound writer, calls it the mindset, heartset, soulset, and healthset. Same thing, different words. Many of the highest achievers, happiest and most successful people have applied these four and have reached their fullest potential. It is one of the greatest realizations we can ever have. This is the type of reality check we all need to hear.

Back to our goals. Do not be vague and make sure to specify exactly what you want to accomplish. Once you have set what you want to do and accomplish, you must begin working on your game plan. Exactly how are you going to start working towards your goals? What measures are you going to take? What do you need to do daily to progress toward them? What sacrifices need to be made? For example, if one of my goals is to be healthier, then I need to start thinking about how I will get there, what I need to do and learn, and what I need to sacrifice. Here is an example of what I would write:

- I need to decrease the amount of bad carbs and fats I am intaking. Decrease consumption of bread and pasta by half. Avoid chips.
- I need to decrease the amount of sweets and sugary foods I consume. Avoid sodas, buying sweets in bulk and processed snacks. Natural is better.
- Substitute cravings for sweets for Nature's Candy. Go to the grocery store 2x a week to stock up on some apples, nectarines, peaches, carrots, cucumbers and sugar snap peas.
- Start to exercise more frequently. I will find genuine and real fitness influencers who help inspire me to become my best self and research what they seem to be doing.

- I will stop going out to eat as much. I will start saying no to my friends who ask me to go out to eat with them.
- I will reward myself with my favorite indulgences once every other day. I will consume my rewards in moderation.

Make sure to look at your plan a couple of times a day to get it ingrained in your mind. I look and envision my life goals every morning and night. When we set goals, we tend to forget about them. Do NOT forget about them! Here's another one:

I want to become a better me by being more loving and forgiving instead of harboring hatred and resentment. My game plan:

- I will seek to understand instead of making assumptions.
- If I catch myself in a position to get angry or resentful, I will become aware of these emotions and try to let them go.
- I will not take anything personally.
- I will practice self-love more, which means saying no to anything that will have the potential of harming me.
- I will confront the person who hurt my feelings instead of keeping it in and gaining resentment.

- I will check up on the people who are closest in my life and show them that I care and love them.
- I will forgive those who I thought were incapable of receiving my forgiveness.

I would strongly recommend for you start becoming more accustomed to being alone, because this is where most of the progress gets made. Cut out the people in your life who are stuck in a mindset of mediocrity and normality. If you want to rise, you cannot associate yourself with people who will either bring you down or who won't raise you up. If that means spending more time by yourself, then by all means, that is what you should do. It's time to start fresh and begin a new chapter of your life. This should feel exciting and liberating.

Dump that toxic boyfriend or girlfriend. Spend less time with your negative uncle or avoid him completely. Do not be stagnant. Remove yourself from situations that will hurt you mentally, emotionally and spiritually. Stop hanging out with people who don't show any signs of wanting to improve their well-being, look at their actions over their words. Put an end to partying every weekend night and binge drinking. Don't check your phone after waking up or before going to bed. Turn off the noise. Turn off the chaos. No more one-sided relationships, you deserve better - enough of letting people treat you like a doormat.

Time to Work

Start waking up early and getting your work done. Begin setting new goals, dreams and aspirations. Become the person that you want to manifest in your life as a friend or a future spouse. Reach for the stars. Remove the insecurities, doubts and fears. Shut up the negative Nancy in your head. Be nice to everyone. Love and forgive the people who hate on you. Reach out to people in need. Give to people who are less fortunate. Read more. Pray more. Meditate more. Quiet your mind more. Implement a successful early morning routine. Quit whatever you feel like doesn't resonate with you. Be grateful for things you usually take for granted like your breath or your five senses. Love. Love. Love. Wake up each day and say, "thank you." Do what you are afraid of doing. Ask people how they are doing. Move. Move. And move. Get your creative juices flowing. Live. Enjoy living.

Never stop learning, growing and thriving. Stagnation will never progress you and it is the catalyst for a life not well lived! Here are some of my favorite and highly recommended books to read:

1. *Outwitting the Devil* by Napoleon Hill
2. *Mastery of Self* by Don Miguel Ruiz
3. *Power of No* by Claudia and James Altucher
4. *5am Club: Own Your Morning. Elevate Your Life* by Robin Sharma
5. *The Miracle Morning* by Hal Elrod

6. *The Mastery of Love* by Don Miguel Ruiz
7. *Think and Grow Rich* by Napoleon Hill
8. *Rich Dad Poor Dad* by Robert Kiyosaki
9. *Captivating: Unveiling the Mystery of a Woman's Soul* by John and Stasi Eldredge
10. *This I Know for Sure* by Oprah Winfrey
11. *How to Win Friends and Influence People* by Dale Carnegie

In May of 2019, my coach and I were going over the 5-year plan I wrote. I was reading it aloud and told him that I would definitely want to write a book by that 5-year mark because I felt that I lacked the intelligence and knowledge to do it now. He replied saying something along the lines of, "uh, why not just start it today? You have what it takes." My reaction was like "what did you just say? I can't do that!" I thought I wasn't good enough and didn't possess enough knowledge. I thought, "who am I, a 19-year-old girl, to write a book?" But the other part of me got extremely stirred up, I had that wave of stimulation hitting me like it always does when an idea comes up. That part of me won, like it always does. The day after that I began writing.

Ironically, that was actually one of my 2019 goals that I set a couple of days before 2018 ended. After writing all of my goals, the last one that I wrote down was, "maybe write a book?" I knew that I probably wasn't going to do it.

It was all a part of God's plan, and I didn't even know it at the time. He has a funny way of working sometimes.

This book contains a lot of advice on how to live a better life, mainly focusing on young adults, but honestly, anyone can learn from the advice given. Some people will take this advice and transform it into wonder, others won't do anything about it. That's okay, I believe that everyone experiences everything at different times of their lives for a reason. But just remember, it's always better to start earlier.

Beautiful things happen when you take a giant leap of faith and begin working on yourself for *yourself.* Remember Napoleon Hill's quote, "Our only limitations are those we set up in our own minds." Most people have let their fear or doubt overcome their desire, which is exactly why only a small fraction of people are successful in the world.

The system is not against you. Don't blame the government or your parents. Don't rely on a lottery win or an opportunity to fall on your lap that will propel you into prosperity. Last but not least, the inherent qualities you were born with don't play a role in the way you turn out. Excuses create self-sabotage. For every problem you have in your life, there has been someone else that has conquered it and won. If nobody else will tell you, then I will.

We are only at the beginning, ladies and gentlemen. The journey won't be easy, but the rewards are worth it. Always remember the four bodies we must work on and master to become our best selves: emotional, mental, spiritual and physical. Along with that, remember the success formula: dedication, determination, discipline and faith = greatness. Apply this in your daily life.

As we close off this book, I want to thank all of you for picking it up and reading it. I truly hope that at least one thing that I wrote really resonated with you. From the bottom of my heart, I really do mean it when I say you are capable of anything. You just need to unlock that capability and start running with it. I got this, you got this, *we* got this.

God bless,
Nastassia Ponomarenko